I0820536

THE GOSPEL OF JOHN

LIVES OF GREAT RELIGIOUS BOOKS

For a full list of titles in the series, go to https://press.princeton.edu/series/lives-of-great-religious-books

The Gospel of John, Kim Haines-Eitzen

Paradise Lost, Alan Jacobs

The Jefferson Bible, Peter Manseau

The Passover Haggadah, Vanessa L. Ochs

Josephus's *The Jewish War,* Martin Goodman

The *Song of Songs,* Ilana Pardes

The Life of Saint Teresa of Avila, Carlos Eire

The Book of *Exodus,* Joel S. Baden

The Book of *Revelation,* Timothy Beal

The *Talmud,* Barry Scott Wimpfheimer

The *Koran* in English, Bruce B. Lawrence

The *Lotus Sūtra,* Donald S. Lopez, Jr.

John Calvin's *Institutes of the Christian Religion,* Bruce Gordon

C. S. Lewis's *Mere Christianity,* George M. Marsden

The *Bhagavad Gita,* Richard H. Davis

The *Yoga Sutra of Patanjali,* David Gordon White

Thomas Aquinas's *Summa theologiae,* Bernard McGinn

The *Book of Common Prayer,* Alan Jacobs

The Book of *Job,* Mark Larrimore

The *Dead Sea Scrolls,* John J. Collins

The Book of *Genesis,* Ronald Hendel

The Gospel of John

A BIOGRAPHY

KIM HAINES-EITZEN

PRINCETON UNIVERSITY PRESS
PRINCETON & OXFORD

Published by Princeton University Press
41 William Street, Princeton, New Jersey 08540
99 Banbury Road, Oxford OX2 6JX

press.princeton.edu

GPSR Authorized Representative: Easy Access System Europe - Mustamäe tee 50, 10621 Tallinn, Estonia, gpsr.requests@easproject.com

ISBN 9780691235257
ISBN (e-book) 9780691235264

British Library Cataloging-in-Publication Data is available

Editorial: Fred Appel and Tara Dugan
Production Editorial: Nathan Carr
Jacket/Cover Design: Wanda España
Production: Erin Suydam
Publicity: Maria Whelan and Charlotte Coyne
Copyeditor: Anne Sanow

Jacket image: PAINTING / Alamy Stock Photo

This book has been composed in Arno

Printed in the United States of America

10 9 8 7 6 5 4 3 2 1

For my father
and in memory of my mother

Stories are everywhere. Stories are *us*.
It's story that makes us human.

—WILL STORR

CONTENTS

PREFACE

IN THE very first chapter of the Gospel of John, Nathanael asks a simple question: Can anything good come out of Nazareth? He seems utterly incredulous that Jesus, the one prophesied by scripture, could come from this tiny, backwater, virtually unknown village. The question hovers over the whole Gospel. The implied answer is, of course, unequivocally yes. In many ways, the Fourth Gospel can be read as one long extended and emphatic affirmative: it's not just something good that came out of Nazareth, according to the narrator, but something divine.

It's a question I myself have wondered about many times, in part because I grew up in Nazareth. By the early 1970s, it had grown from a village to a small city whose residents were mostly Muslim and Christian. The Christian presence was especially felt in the many churches and pilgrimage sites associated with the life of Jesus. Hundreds of tourists arrived daily to visit Mary's Well, the Church of the Annunciation and the ruins beneath it, St. Joseph's Church, and what's known as the "Synagogue Church," a small medieval church built on the purported ruins of Jesus's own synagogue. And on the hospital compound where we lived and in the elementary school where we learned Arabic.

As a child, I don't remember worrying too much about the intricate and complex tensions between history and tradition. Who knew, after all, what exactly happened where? Who really knew what happened, period? Did it matter if this or that site was *really* the place where a story took place? For me, Nazareth was both utterly normal, my home, and endlessly fascinating. We loved to watch the many buses arrive, and, as the tourists spilled out into the sunshine, we tried to guess where they were from based on their outfits, especially their hats. There was something contagious about their excitement. Their awe.

I would never have guessed that I would go on to become a historian of early Christianity and early Judaism (and I don't think my parents would have either). Archaeological sites struck me as commonplace and boring (and hot!). We walked past Mary's Well every day on the way to and from school, shopped in the souk next to the Church of the Annunciation. And the villages around Nazareth? We drove through these to get to places far more interesting to me: the sea of Galilee or Sakhne, where we could go swimming. I must have been told, probably many times, that the village of Kafr Kenna was named for biblical Cana, where Jesus turned water into wine at a wedding according to the Gospel of John. I'm sure we would have visited the so-called Wedding Church there. There was always a sense of history around us.

As I've been writing this book, I've been going through my father's substantial slide collection of Jordan, Egypt, and Palestine/Israel from the 1950s, 60s, 70s. I'm struck by the slides of Mount Gerizim and the village of Balata (Shechem)—locations associated with the Samaritans and the story of the Samaritan woman in John 4. In one of them, crowds have gathered on the slopes of the mountain for the Samaritan Passover celebration. And then there are pictures of the traditional tomb of Lazarus, whose resurrection story is told only in the Gospel of John. The tomb and the more modern church of Mary, Martha, and Lazarus are located in Bethany near Jerusalem. The dome of the church looks still new in the slides, its sheen a bright silver. And the church's pale limestone façade with three colorful mosaic panels, each with a figure from the story, stands in stark contrast to the deep blue sky. In one slide, the church's dome is shown directly next to the minaret of the local mosque, a pairing I'm sure my father wanted to capture. I study these and I try to remember the experiences I had as a child.

Of course, photographs are no more reliable than memory when it comes to history, to the events of the past. Both are built from layers of experience, selection, framing, and perception. My father used his slides to illustrate ideas and to recount stories, and while there is something fixed about the images—for example, place and time—they also reveal and require interpretation. The moment we encounter an image, we begin to interpret it, to explain it. We conjure up words and stories that help us make sense of images. And the same is true of how we read texts. The process is endlessly dynamic: we bring our memories and experiences to bear on our interpretations, which in turn help us to make sense of the world.

When I look now at the slides of limestone and olive groves, churches and mosques, mountains and tombs and ruins, I am reminded of the stories I was told over and over about what happened here, what may have happened there. In spite of my childhood disinterest in history and, yes, the many archaeological sites, I realize that the experience of seeing the past visible in the landscape around us lit my imagination. I found freedom in imagining, a world of possibility. Who knows? What if? These questions still intrigue and inspire me. There is so much we do not know about history—something I repeat throughout this book. I'm a historian, not a theologian, and whenever possible I try to reconstruct events of the past based on available and reliable evidence. But for much, if not all, of the Gospel of

John, we simply do not have the kinds of sources we need to speak with assurance about what did and didn't happen.

This book is in many ways about the vibrancy of the human imagination. About the life of stories, the way they matter to us, the way they puzzle and mystify us, the way we tell and retell them. Although the narrator of John's Gospel speaks with confidence, even insistence, about events and teachings, Nathanael's surprise can be felt throughout. *Can* anything good come out of Nazareth? Such a question, of course, is not frozen in time. I haven't visited Nazareth in many years now, in part because the political situation is simply too maddening, too heartbreaking. To dwell in the world of imagination sometimes requires distance.

For nearly two thousand years, the Gospel of John has captured the imagination of commentators and composers, artists and activists, preachers and politicians, monks and missionaries. The long legacy of interpretation, imagination, and religious conviction is challenging and, at times, downright offensive. But above all, it reminds us that stories have lives of their own: we cannot control their interpretation or their unruly afterlives. They serve, instead, as enduring witnesses to the potent vitality of the human imagination.

Introduction

EVERY SPRING, Christians around the world gather to celebrate Easter. Music of various kinds accompanies the observance of Easter as well as the somber services of the preceding Holy Week. But the performance of one piece always seems to invite controversy: Johann Sebastian Bach's *St. John Passion*, a choral and orchestral work first performed on Good Friday, April 7, 1724. Take, for example, the Cleveland Orchestra's performance of Bach's *St. John Passion* in the spring of 2017 or, that same spring, five performances of the work staged in New York City by different orchestras and choral groups. Each of these performances was accompanied by debate among community members: Should the piece continue to be performed? Is it ethical to perform it? To listen to it? Conductors now frequently hold panel discussions to explain the work and to counter opposition. And yet performances of the *St. John Passion* continue to be contentious.

At stake in the controversy about Bach's *St. John Passion* is not the music per se, which is often regarded as one of the pinnacles of Bach's compositional career. Rather, the controversies stem in large part from the text of the choral work—in particular, the passages from the Gospel of John that Bach chose to incorporate into the choral work—and the manner in which Bach's music heightened the problematic text. Bach used the German translation of the Gospel of John—the translation done by Martin Luther during the sixteenth-century Reformation—and its narratives of the trial and death of Jesus. It is in this translation of the Gospel, as well as in its Greek original, that we can locate the heart of the controversy, for it is in the Gospel of John that "the Jews" "cry out" ever more urgently "crucify, crucify him." Identifying the crowds calling for Jesus's execution specifically as "the Jews" is distinctive to this Gospel and audiences, performers, and critics alike have long questioned whether the apparent antisemitism in the *St. John Passion* should make us rethink performances of the work.

Such debates illustrate just one of the many legacies not of Bach, Luther specifically, or the history of antisemitism, but of the Gospel of John itself. Likely written sometime in the last decade of the first century, perhaps around 95 CE, the Gospel of John is unique among all of the canonical and noncanonical Gospels. John's differences from the Synoptic Gospels (Matthew, Mark, and Luke) are striking: it begins not with the birth narrative, but with a poetic reinvention of the beginnings of the Book of Genesis, one that places Jesus as logos, the Word, in the beginning of creation. In this Gospel, Jesus does not teach in parables; he teaches openly about his identity (e.g., "I am the light of the world"); his healings are not kept secret, but rather presented as open signs of his identity. This Gospel alone contains the well-known stories of the water changed into wine in Cana, the raising of Lazarus, the woman taken in adultery, and many others; images such as Jesus as the good shepherd, the "Lamb of God," the "word made flesh"—these are unique to John. It is in this Gospel that we meet, too, the disciple "whom Jesus loved"—the character of the never-named, mysterious "beloved disciple" who is said to have recorded the words found in this Gospel. And it is in the Gospel of John that "the Jews"—as a collective—are depicted in strident opposition to Jesus. Here they are unequivocally responsible for Jesus's execution.

It is in part due to these distinctive features that the Gospel of John has had such a long and paradoxical biography. Throughout Christian history, the Gospel of John has been the most "beloved" of all the Gospels—a Gospel highly regarded for its "soaring," "glorious," and "spiritual" qualities. Its language, stories, and images lie at the forefront of late ancient Christological controversies, divisions between Eastern and Western Christianity, the Crusades and Reformation, and modern evangelical movements. The first biblical commentary written by a Christian was one written on the Gospel of John; among the very earliest manuscripts of Christian texts is a second-century fragment of the Gospel of John; John was a centerpiece for Augustine's works of theology and biblical interpretation; Johannine ideas about the "word made flesh" and "signs" became important to the debates about icons and the use of images in the early Middle Ages; crusaders drew upon passages from John to justify their conquests of Jerusalem; Protestant reformers privileged the Gospel of John above other Gospels; and so on. This is without a doubt the Christian Gospel with the greatest impact throughout history—and this history can be charted by its beloved and benighted status. It is a contentious history.

Perhaps it was inevitable that a Gospel animated by paradox and stark oppositions would have a thwarted afterlife: light and dark, spirit and flesh, those from above and those below, of the world and not of the world, believers and nonbelievers, insiders and outsiders, truth knowers and the ignorant, the Jews and Jesus's followers, the saved and sinners, the living and the dead—the striking distinctions and dualistic language running throughout this Gospel have born richly dynamic and deeply problematic reverberations. The history of the Gospel of John takes us to the heights of Christian theology and the cultivation of the very crux of Christian identity while simultaneously drawing our attention to the complex and challenging impact the Gospel has had in religious history and on the global stage.

In this book, I tell the story of this complex history not to judge the Gospel or the merits of various theological views on the Gospel, but to understand how and why the Gospel of John has had a such an important legacy. In the coming chapters, we will begin with the earliest history of the Gospel—its origins in the first century, questions about its author(s) and first readers, the transmission and dissemination of the Gospel as a book. We will examine how the stories from the Gospel have been rendered in art and film, as well as in music; how John's unique stories and language have intersected with major developments in Christian history like the medieval Crusades, the Protestant Reformation, and modern evangelical movements. My goal is to the tell the story of the book itself, while also attending to the many ways that the legacy of this gospel exceeds its existence as a book. It is important to keep in mind that when the Gospel of John was written and indeed throughout much of history, the vast majority of people could not read or write, so their encounters with the text was through listening to it read or, probably more frequently, hearing the stories found in the Gospel told and retold in predominantly oral societies.

Throughout this book, I will variously call this Gospel the Fourth Gospel, because of its placement in the New Testament following the Gospels of Matthew, Mark, and Luke. At times, for simplicity, I will call it John, but at the outset I should emphasize that the Gospel was written anonymously and the title and tradition associating it with Jesus's disciple John, the son of Zebedee, emerged after its composition. We will look more closely at the question of authorship, but I will continue to emphasize how much we do not know about the person or persons who wrote the book. Another term will appear quite frequently in the following chapters, and that is the term "Johannine," a term used by scholars to identify the ideology and literary characteristics of the Gospel of John and the three canonical epistles of John (1, 2, and 3 John). Encountering this Gospel as a book is only one way to think of its history; the Gospel of John has had a legacy that goes well beyond its book form: everything from the earliest paintings of stories from the Gospel to contemporary billboards, film, and music show us that this Gospel has had numerous and varied afterlives.

For now, the place to begin is by setting the historical stage for the story of the Fourth Gospel.

Setting the Stage

Why was the Gospel of John originally written in Greek? This might seem odd, given that Jesus's native language was Aramaic. There is a simple answer: the conquests of Alexander, King of Macedon, who, in the fourth century BCE, began a military campaign throughout the eastern Mediterranean region, down into Egypt, and then on eastward through to what is modern-day Iraq, Iran, and northern India. Much has been written about Alexander—frequently called Alexander the Great—but for our purposes a few key details are important. First, in the wake of his conquests, the gradual but nearly complete transformation of the eastern Mediterranean regions (and beyond) into a conglomeration of Greek city-states and the spread of Greek language and culture was the beginning of what we can call the

Hellenistic period in Greek and Roman history. It is difficult to overestimate the significance of the spread of Hellenism for the later development of Christianity: all of the texts contained in the New Testament—indeed, all Christian texts that we have from the earliest period—were written in Greek, because by the first century CE, Greek had become the lingua franca throughout the Mediterranean and Near Eastern world. Paul wrote in Greek, the early Christian Gospels were written in Greek, the earliest Church Fathers wrote in Greek, and so forth.

Alongside the gradual change to Greek language as the dominant spoken and literary language came Hellenistic philosophical, religious, and cultural ideas about the pantheon of the Greek gods, sacrificial rituals that were conducted in Greek temples to please these gods, the philosophical writings of Aristotle and Plato, Greek art and music—all of these had enormous impact on the history of Christian origins. It is important, too, to understand that the spread of Hellenism did not wipe out indigenous religions and cultures: we can think of the period as a kind of historical layering or a meshwork of different cultures that came together, which strictly speaking ended with the Roman conquests of the Near East in the first century CE, although the effects of Alexander's conquests continued to shape a Near East now overlaid with Roman ideas and cultures.

For our purposes, beyond the spread of Greek language and culture, one of the most important developments during the period was Hellenism's impact on the history of Judaism. Judaism, as a religion, was born out of ancient Near Eastern Israelite religion—religious practices, ideas, and sacred texts that stretched back into the second millennium BCE. Israelite religion was focused on place—in particular, the regions around Jerusalem, where King Solomon's Temple was built in the tenth century BCE—and the rituals associated with the annual religious-agricultural festivals. Like ancient Near Eastern religions (and Greek and Roman religions), Israelite religious practice included sacrificial rituals. But there were two key ways in which it differed from other ancient Near Eastern and later Greek religions. First, it was monotheistic or, more precisely, henotheistic: the Israelites worshiped one high God, though they acknowledged the existence of other gods. Second, Israelite religion and subsequent Judaism had sacred scriptures—the Torah. These scriptures were written in Hebrew (and Aramaic) and they tell the story of the history of the Israelites from the creation of the world down to the destruction of the Solomonic Temple by the Babylonians in 586 BCE—an event with tremendous significance for the development of Judaism. The Babylonians exiled many of the residents of Jerusalem and the surrounding area to Babylonia, sparking what we call the diaspora, the spread of Judaism around the Mediterranean and Near East; it had begun earlier, of course, but the Babylonian conquest and exile accelerated and expanded Jewish diaspora.

The scriptures also told the story of the reconstruction of the Jerusalem Temple under the Persians and a return of some of the exiles. This new Jerusalem Temple, completed in the late sixth century BCE, is what scholars call the Second Temple and after extensive renovations by King Herod centuries later it was the Temple that was standing in Jesus's day . The sacrificial rituals in the Temple and the sacred books of Moses (Genesis, Exodus, Leviticus, Numbers, and Deuteronomy), the prophets (like Isaiah and Jeremiah and many others), and an assortment of other writings, such as the book of Psalms—these were important for Jewish identity.

Much of what I have described here predates Alexander the Great: conquest and exile had already shaped Judaism by the time of Alexander. But what happens to Judaism in the wake of

Alexander's conquests is dramatic: communities of Jews, now residing throughout the Near East, gradually began adopting the Greek language; eventually they translated the Hebrew scriptures into Greek, and they began worshipping in synagogues, which were not places of sacrificial rituals like the Temple in Jerusalem, but rather places for prayer and study and for communal gatherings. The word itself, "synagogue," came from the Greek *synagō*, which meant "to gather together." The origin of synagogues remains somewhat murky: some may have been built prior to Alexander, but our best archaeological evidence for synagogues comes from the Hellenistic period and later. These early synagogues were, as far as we can tell, fairly small structures, with seating around the sides of the building and a Torah niche/cupboard to hold the scrolls of scripture.

For the most part, Jews were permitted to continue practicing their religious rituals like the sacrifices in the Jerusalem Temple and to gather in synagogues in the Hellenistic period. But one of the things we find during this time is that Judaism became increasingly diverse because, in part, Hellenism was viewed differently by different Jewish communities. Some communities seem to have embraced Hellenism fully and used the Greek translation of the Hebrew Bible (called the Septuagint) as their Bible. Some Jews attended Greek schools and participated in Greek life, including even religious festivals or the Greek games. Others, however, resisted such changes.[1] It's in the Hellenistic period that we see the development of a variety of Jewish groups: the Pharisees, the teachers of Jewish law and interpreters of scripture; the Sadducees, priests officiating at the Temple sacrifices in Jerusalem; the Essenes, who opposed the Sadducean priests and appear to have left Jerusalem to form a community on the northwest shores of the Dead Sea, to whom the Dead Sea Scrolls are linked; and later the Zealots, who wanted to take up arms against Roman rule.

These developments happened gradually, but they came to shape Jewish history in significant ways, including during the aftermath of the destruction of the second Jerusalem Temple by the Romans in 70 CE. Sometimes there were Jewish revolts against Greek or Roman rule: in the second century BCE, for example, the Maccabean revolt, and the Jewish revolt of the late 60s CE. One of the fascinating developments within Judaism appears to have its origin during such revolts: an ideology or worldview we call "apocalypticism"—a word that comes from the Greek word *apokalypsis*, which meant "revelation." This is the idea that the world is currently dominated by evil forces and good folks are being oppressed, but the tides will change—there will be a judgment day when evil rulers will be crushed and the devout will be vindicated. Parts of the Book of Daniel, in the Hebrew Bible, were written in the second century BCE and offer us a particularly illuminating example of early Jewish apocalypticism: a vision, a revelation, of beasts rising out of the sea comes to the prophet Daniel, and as he watches he sees "thrones were set in place, and an Ancient One took his throne, his clothing was white as snow, and the hair of his head like pure wool . . . the court sat in judgment, and the books were opened" (Daniel 7: 9–10). Daniel keeps watching the scene unfold: "I saw one," he says, "like a human being, coming with the clouds of heaven . . . to him was given dominion and glory and kingship" (7:13–14). It's important to understand that the phrase "one like a human being" can also be translated "one like a son of man."

The title "son of man" will eventually be used by some of the earliest followers of Jesus, who saw him as the awaited messiah, the anointed one, the figure who was prophesied by Daniel and others, the one who would rescue the Jewish people from their suffering. Here is why setting this stage becomes so essential to understanding the Fourth Gospel, as well as all of the early Christian Gospels. These texts were written in the first century in a world of Jews, Zoroastrians, Greeks, and Romans—a complex religious and political landscape with a long history of domination and resistance, and, in the case of Judaism, a sacred scripture that explained catastrophic events like exile and the destruction of the Temple in Jerusalem. And this history is fundamental to understanding the historical Jesus and his earliest Jewish followers: when we reconstruct the history of Jesus's life and teachings from the sources available, many scholars have argued that he was an apocalyptic Jewish itinerant preacher, and that he gathered followers who shared his sense of a coming judgment day and a new kingdom of God, a new kingdom that would rise up after the evil oppressors had been destroyed.

The reconstruction of the historical Jesus is beyond the scope of our study of the Fourth Gospel; there are many treatments of this period and Jesus's life and teachings.[2] It is also beyond the goals of this book to say whether or not the Fourth Gospel got history right, or whether its story of Jesus is accurate. But I want to signal here something that is important for understanding the Fourth Gospel, which was written after the destruction of the Jewish Temple in 70 CE: we should read the Gospel not for whether it gets history "right" but for what it reveals about the complex time period in which it was written. The fact that it was written in Greek, but uses some Aramaic terms, is important; when the Gospel of John quotes passages from the Hebrew Bible, it does so from the Septuagint, the Greek translation; when it fashions an opposition between Jesus and, say, the Pharisees, it does so from an understanding of the complexity of Jewish history; and when it softens apocalyptic ideas, it does so from an awareness that the judgment day that Daniel (and Jesus) seem to have predicted had not yet happened.

This brief historical survey will be important in the coming chapters. For now, we need to attend to what we mean by the term "gospel" and how and why some Gospels came to be included in the canon of the New Testament. Then, we'll turn to the many ways that the Gospel of John is distinctive from other ancient Gospels.

What Is a Gospel?

The term "gospel" comes from an Old English word, which was itself a translation of an ancient Greek word, *euaggelion* (with the "gg" pronounced as "ng" in English, like *euangelion*), which meant simply "good news" or a "good report." A friend or relative, for example, might bring you "good news" or a send a "good report." The Greek *euaggelion* is also where we get our terms "evangelist," "evangelical," and "evangelism"; the Gospel writers have long been called the Evangelists, the Protestant Reformers in the sixteenth century were called Evangelicals, and the work of missionary forms of Christianity support evangelism—the spread of the "good news." If we want to get into the weeds with etymology, it might be useful to add that the prefix *eu* in Greek meant "good" and the term *aggelos* (from which we get our English word "angel") meant "message" or "messenger." In its earliest use by Christians, the term *euaggelion* referred to a message—the Christian message, or "good news," about Jesus, his resurrection, and salvation. The term was not necessarily attached to anything written down, such as a text or a book. We have largely lost this meaning in English. When we hear something called "the gospel truth," for example, it means a belief or message that can be believed and relied upon—something that is true and accurate.

In the second century, the term *euaggelion* comes to be used by Christians to refer to a book—in particular, a book that claims to tell the story of Jesus. The message or gospel of Jesus now becomes the story of Jesus as told in a Gospel. This is how we wind up with our common understanding that a Gospel is a book and, more specifically, a book about the figure Jesus. The form that early Christian Gospels took varied: some were simply a collection of sayings of Jesus with little narrative as we find in the Gospel of Thomas; others told the story of Jesus from his birth through to his execution and resurrection as we find in the Gospels of Luke and Matthew. We might think of a Gospel in this sense as a kind of ancient biography of Jesus, but very few early Christian gospels narrate the story of Jesus's life in the way we might think of a modern biography with, for example, the story of birth, childhood, education, adulthood, and death; the historical context of the individual's life; the influences that led them to become a figure worthy of a biography; and so forth.

We have surprisingly few stories of Jesus as a child in any of the early Christian Gospels—the exceptions here are the story of Jesus in the Temple of Jerusalem when he was twelve years old as found in the Gospel of Luke and the stories of a young Jesus found in the Infancy Gospel of Thomas. We hear very little about Jesus's family and we do not encounter explanations of the historical and contextual influences that led to Jesus's life as a teacher or preacher. These Gospels were not written as neutral accounts of Jesus's life. Instead, early Christian Gospels were invested in persuading their readers—and their listeners—of who Jesus was and the meaning and significance of his life, death, and resurrection. And this is why it is so critical to understand each Gospel as a distinct rendering of the story of Jesus, a story meant to persuade the reader of Jesus's identity. No two Gospels were exactly the same. Some authors wanted to emphasize Jesus as a Jewish prophet; others portrayed him as a teacher of esoteric and secret wisdom. Some Gospels presented Jesus as a teacher and healer, while others stressed his divinity.

Early Christian writers knew that there were different stories of Jesus circulating. They knew that written Gospels told different stories; that some told the same stories in different ways; and that some outright contradicted one another. The Gospel of Luke actually begins with a disclaimer of sorts: "Since many have undertaken to set down an orderly account of the events that have been fulfilled among us, just as they were handed on to us by those who from the beginning were eyewitnesses and servants of the word, I too decided, after investigating everything carefully from the very first, to write an orderly account" (Lk 1:1–3).[3] The Gospel of John ends by suggesting that there were "many other things that Jesus did," and all the books in the world could not contain them (Jn 21:25). Each Gospel writer deliberately selected the material to include and shaped the story to convey a particular message.

Attending here to the chronology of Christian origins helps us understand the context of these diverse Gospels. The oral accounts about Jesus's life and teaching first came to be written down some thirty or forty years after his death. It is widely accepted among scholars that the historical Jesus lived from roughly 4 BCE to 29 CE. The social and historical context of Jesus's life was early first-century Palestine, his language was Aramaic, and he was Jewish. These three aspects of Jesus's life—date, context, and language—are critical to remember when we look at the Gospels, all of which were written in Greek, and almost certainly not in Palestine nor by eyewitnesses of the accounts they tell. Among the Gospels that have survived, the Gospel of Mark is likely the earliest, written sometime between the late 60s or early 70s CE. But Gospels then proliferated: the Gospels of Matthew, Luke, John, Thomas, Peter, and many others began to be written and circulated during the late first century and throughout the second and third centuries.

As we will see, there are important distinctions to be made between the history of the Gospel of John and the Christian traditions about the Gospel. Traditions sprang up around the Mediterranean world about what happened to Jesus's apostles: for example, Christian tradition claims that the apostle James was buried in Spain at Santiago de Compostela Cathedral, Peter and Paul buried in Rome (Peter in St. Peter's Basilica in Vatican City and Paul in the Basilica of St. Paul Outside the Walls), and Thomas was said to have traveled to India and he is now venerated in San Thome Basilica in Chennai. According to the most widespread Christian tradition, the Fourth Gospel was written by one of Jesus's disciples, John, also known as one of the sons of Zebedee. Tradition associated him with Ephesus in Asia Minor and in the fifth or sixth century a basilica was built there to commemorate him. The remains of this basilica, which was constructed around his supposed tomb, along with its baptismal pool, can still be visited today near the town of Selçuk in western Turkey.

We will return to traditions about John's author in chapter 7, which deals with the "beloved disciple" in the Gospel of John, for over time this character came to be identified as John, the son of Zebedee, the author of the Fourth Gospel. Tradition also associated this same "John" as the one who wrote the Book of Revelation, though its style of writing, ideology, and apocalyptic content is quite different from the Gospel of John. For now, it is critical that we distinguish this tradition from the historical

FIGURE I.1. St. John Basilica with the tomb of St. John in the foreground, Ephesus, Turkey. Credit: Author.

record: even if the Gospel of John had its origins in the oral stories of Jesus's followers, the final writing and editing of the Gospel took place in the very late first century, long after Jesus's followers would have died, and it is written in Greek, not the language that Jesus and his first followers spoke, which was Aramaic.

An Emerging Christian Canon

Given how many Gospels were written by Christians, it is worthwhile asking how only four Gospels made it into the canon of the New Testament, and how and why the Gospel of John came to be one of them. The earliest Christians inherited from their Jewish origins a concept of scripture—sacred and authoritative texts. The canon of Jewish scriptures consisted of the five books of Moses (Genesis, Exodus, Leviticus, Numbers, and Deuteronomy), prophetic books (e.g., those of Isaiah, Jeremiah, Amos, Hosea, and others), and a diverse set of other writings, including the book of Psalms and the Song of Solomon. These scriptures were written in Hebrew and subsequently translated into Greek, a translation called the Septuagint, as I've already indicated. One might think that having these scriptures would suffice for early Christians, but as Christianity began to develop increasingly apart from its Jewish origins, Christians turned to some of the earliest texts written by believers in the Jesus movement—texts like the letters of Paul and the various Gospels written in the late first century. Over time, these works came to be understood as scripture—a New Testament—on par with the Jewish scriptures, which Christians now called the Old Testament.

There have been many treatments of the complex process of canonization in early Christianity.[4] For our purposes, it is important simply to note that the formation of a Christian canon of scripture—a Christian Bible—took place over the course of hundreds of years. The Greek word *kanōn* probably derived from an Aramaic word for "reed" and specifically a papyrus reed, usually, that was used for measuring—much like we think of a ruler or measuring stick. Paul, for example, uses the term in some of his letters and there the meaning is a kind of rule, standard, or norm; and, subsequently, it meant more specifically a "rule of faith." But in the fourth century, the term comes to be used by Christians to refer to a collection of Christian writings, the Christian canon of scripture. It is not until the late fourth century, some 350 years after Jesus's life, however, that we find a bishop (Athanasius in Alexandria, Egypt) writing a list of New Testament books that accords with the New Testament today.

The impetus for the closure of a canon of scriptures came in response to a diversity of Christian beliefs and practices. And our only sources for these developments come from the writings of Christians who were concerned about "right belief." Closing a canon of scriptures became, then, one strategy toward unity in the debates over heresy and orthodoxy.

As early as the late second century, a bishop named Irenaeus from what is now southern France wrote the following:

> Matthew also issued a written Gospel among the Hebrews in their own dialect, while Peter and Paul were preaching at Rome, and laying the foundations of the Church. After their departure, Mark, the disciple and interpreter of Peter, did also hand down to us in writing what had been preached by Peter. Luke also, the companion of Paul, recorded in a book the Gospel preached by him. Afterwards, John, the disciple of the Lord, who also had leaned upon His breast, did himself publish a Gospel during his residence at Ephesus in Asia. (Irenaeus, *Against Heresies* 3.1)

We will return to Irenaeus in chapter 3, but for now it is worth noting how he identifies the four gospels and emphasizes the importance of these four gospels—no more and no fewer belong in the sacred scriptures, he argues. As he writes against those he perceives as heretics, Irenaeus claims there are four gospels alone that contain the right belief. And the number four is significant, for, he says, there are "four zones of the world in which we live, and four principal winds"; the gospels are like "four pillars, breathing out immortality on every side"; and the four gospels provide "four aspects, but bound together by one Spirit" (*Against Heresies* 3.8). It is worth dwelling on this word "aspects," because Irenaeus here is suggesting that the Gospels tell different stories, provide different perspectives on the figure of Jesus. He acknowledges that the Gospels are different from one another. And yet by putting them side by side in the list of scripture, he seeks to soften those differences and appeals to the idea that in spite of differences, they are "bound together by one Spirit." What had been a fairly fluid state of a variety of Christian Gospels circulating among small Christian communities throughout the Mediterranean will gradually coalesce around the Gospels of Matthew, Mark, Luke, and John as the only canonical Gospels.

One of the important ways to understand the distinctive story that the Fourth Gospel tells is to compare it to the other Gospels contained in the New Testament. By looking closely at John in comparison to the Gospels of Matthew, Mark, and Luke, we can begin to unravel the earliest history of this gospel.

John and the Synoptics

As I have already suggested, each of the early Christian Gospels, including both those that were eventually canonized (i.e., Matthew, Mark, Luke, and John) as well as those that were not (e.g., Thomas, Mary Magdalene, Judas, and others), has distinctive features. And it is in part through each Gospel's particularity that we are able to discern how each Gospel seeks to make a claim about Jesus's identity. This is especially true in the case of the Gospel of John, which stands apart from what have long been called the Synoptic Gospels (Matthew, Mark, and Luke). These three Gospels share much of the same material and, at times, have extensive word-for-word identical material. They are called "Synoptic" because they can be viewed together: in Greek, *syn* means together and *optic* derives from the Greek verb "to see." Yes, each of the Synoptics has its own particular slant on the story of Jesus, but they share similar structures and stories and have many passages in common.

A brief overview of these three Gospels will help us see how John is distinct from them. Two of the Synoptic Gospels (Matthew and Luke) begin with Jesus's birth narrative, though told with different details; they all include the story of Jesus's baptism, and his subsequent teaching in Galilee. In these Gospels, Jesus uses parables to teach—parables are short narratives akin to riddles and they are meant to teach Jesus's followers about the kingdom of God, about ethics, and about following Jesus. A good example is the parable of the sower, found in the Synoptic Gospels, where Jesus says,

> Listen! A sower went out to sow. And as he sowed, some seed fell on the path, and the birds came and ate it up. Other seed fell on rocky ground, where it did not have much soil, and it sprang up quickly, since it had no depth of soil. And when the sun rose, it was scorched; and since it had no root, it withered away. Other seed fell among thorns, and the thorns grew up and choked it, and it yielded no grain. Other seed fell into good soil and brought forth grain, growing up and increasing and yielding thirty and sixty and a hundredfold. (Mk 4:3–8; compare Mt 13:3–8; Lk 8:5–8)

Jesus teaches in parables, he says, so that the people "may indeed listen, but not understand" (Mk 4:12). He also teaches about a coming day of judgment, the kingdom of heaven, and the figure of the Son of Man. In the Synoptics, Jesus performs miracles, especially exorcisms (casting out demons) and healings (such as healing the blind or the lame). Very frequently, he urges his disciples and those who witness these healings not to report what they have seen, but to keep quiet. He debates with the Pharisees about matters of Jewish law—about how, for example, to keep the Sabbath. Toward the end of these Gospels, Jesus makes a fateful trip to Jerusalem for the Passover festival. He goes into the Jewish Temple in Jerusalem and creates a ruckus by driving "out those who were selling and those who were buying in the temple; he overturned the tables of the money changers and the seats of those who sold doves" (Mk 11:15). The Jewish authorities in the Jerusalem Temple become alarmed and one of Jesus's disciples, Judas, betrays him to the chief priests. The Roman authorities then put him on trial, crucify him, and then his followers either find the tomb empty (Mark) or they also find a raised Jesus (Matthew and Luke).

Much of this storyline is likely familiar: the birth narratives with their shepherds and magi; the parables of the mustard seed or the lost sheep and the kingdom of heaven; the exorcisms and healings, the "cleansing of the Temple," the trial and crucifixion. What is fascinating is that almost none of this material is in the Gospel of John. For starters, the structure of the Gospel of John is quite different: the text begins with a poetic opening (1:1–18) rather than a birth narrative. It shifts then to a narrative section that tells of Jesus's miracles, which are almost entirely different from those told in the Synoptics and, even more importantly, in this Gospel they are called "signs," and they are performed openly and meant to show who Jesus is. There is no secrecy motif here. Jesus in the Gospel of John does not teach in parables but rather teaches openly about his own identity. It is true that he sometimes speaks metaphorically, but he does not use parables. He travels several times up to Jerusalem for the Passover. During his final trip to Jerusalem, he delivers a lengthy speech, or sermon, about his own identity (14:12–17:26). The next section of the Gospel contains the story of Jesus's betrayal, trial, crucifixion, and resurrection (18:1–20:31) and a final chapter that reads like a coda and contains more resurrection sightings (21).

John's story is distinctive even in the stories he shares with the Synoptics. The Jewish authorities like the chief priests do appear in this Gospel, for example, but John is the only Gospel to use the specific phrase "the Jews" to identify the crowds around Jesus. The so-called cleansing of the Temple in John takes place near the beginning of the Gospel (2:13–22). The miracles that appear in John are far more dramatic than those found in the Synoptics and there is not a single story about an exorcism. Jesus teaches openly and many of his statements are some of the most frequently quoted passages from the Bible, and they often begin with "I am" statements, such as:

> "I am the light of the world" (Jn 8:12).
> "I am the good shepherd" (Jn 10:11).
> "I am the true vine" (Jn 15:1).

In the next chapter, we will take a closer look at the literary aspects of the Fourth Gospel to unpack its unique story and to understand its history in the first century.

The distinctiveness of the Fourth Gospel has been described by New Testament scholar Robert Kysar like this: "The Fourth Gospel is a maverick among the Gospels. It runs free of the perspective presented in Matthew, Mark, and Luke. It is the nonconformist Gospel of the bunch. No wonder that many of the heretical movements in the history of the Christian church have used the Gospel of John as their authority in the New Testament."[5] Kysar's articulation of the distinctiveness of the Gospel of John and his gesture toward its legacy informs this biography, for it is at once a maverick story of Jesus and yet utterly essential for understanding Christian history.

Stories upon Stories

Humans are, as Jonathan Gottschall has written, the "storytelling animal." "Humans are creatures of story," he writes, "so story touches nearly every aspect of our lives."[6] Biographies are one kind of story that we tell, write, and read. We are endlessly curious to know about others' lives, their challenges and successes, the influences who made them become who they are. At their core, ancient Gospels tell stories. They are biographies, though they lack elements we have come to expect in a biography; they are narratives, though the plot often takes second place to the message. They were written to share with readers and listeners what their writers already knew. Story was essential to the Jesus movement, to the formation of the Christian Gospels, and to the spread of Christianity itself. One of the most effective ways to spread the "good news," after all, was to tell the stories of Jesus's miracles, the many that he healed, and the tale of his own resurrection. Stories abounded, much as they do today. Indeed, "stories are everywhere," as Will Storr claims: "Stories are *us*. It's story that makes us human."[7]

The lines between fact and fiction, between history and literature, are never clear. The Gospel of John in this sense is no different from other ancient Gospels: it is written with a tone of assurance and a conviction its truths, and yet it also crafts a story—a story meant to persuade its readers of Jesus's identity and significance. As Alan Culpepper has argued, "In reading the gospel, one is drawn into a literary world created by the author from materials drawn from life and history as well as imagination and reflection."[8] In telling its story, the Fourth Gospel reveals another story: the story of the communities that called this Gospel scripture. In that sense, the Gospel provides a story within a story, much as this book about the legacy of the Fourth Gospel tells stories within stories. Let's start at the beginning.

1

"In the Beginning"

THE MAKING OF THE GOSPEL OF JOHN

READING THE Gospel of John—indeed, reading any of the early Christian Gospels—requires us to pay close attention to two stories: first, the story of Jesus that the Gospel is telling; second, the story of the later community(ies) whose history is implied by the perspective of the Gospel itself. We read, then, for two layers. There is a rather poor joke that New Testament scholars tell that illustrates this point. It goes like this: "Have you heard that so-and-so has just written an autobiography? The strange thing is, he/she has called it *Jesus of Nazareth*." Such humor serves a purpose, for it reminds us that when we read a Gospel, or when we read any narrative text, we can read it not only for the story it is telling—one, perhaps, set in some distant past or far-off location—but also for what the perspective or approach to the telling might reveal about the author, the author's context, the earliest readers, and so on. Why does the writer tell the story in the specific *way* that he or she does? That's an important question for our understanding of the Fourth Gospel.

In the case of the Gospel of John, a simple timeline may help as we begin a close reading of the Gospel: the historical Jesus lived roughly from 4 BCE to 29 CE. And most scholars assign a date of 90–95 CE for the Gospel of John.[1] There are many reasons for this dating: first, John was written in Greek, which puts it at some distance from the Jesus movement itself; second, the evidence that the Fourth Gospel does not seem to have a good understanding of Palestinian geography suggests it was written from some other location; third, the urgent sense of apocalypticism that we see in the Synoptics is missing from John, which suggests it is written closer to the end of the first century, when we find other Christian writings that seem to be less interested in the idea of an imminent judgment day; and fourth, there are specific clues in the Gospel that suggest it was written after the destruction of the Jerusalem Temple and after some deep rifts had developed between Jesus's followers and the Jewish matrix within which they had been embedded. We have then two contexts, two stories: one is the story of Jesus, set in early first-century Palestine; the other is more obscure but of equal importance, the story of the late first century when the Gospel was probably written.

In this chapter, my goal is first to offer a brief reader's guide to the structure, style, and contents of the Gospel. Then I will turn to some of the key questions and problems scholars have raised about the Gospel, such as its sources. And finally, I will ask how the Gospel reveals the life of a community of Jesus followers that formed during Jesus's life (or just afterward) and grew over the course of the first century—the so-called Johannine community, a community whose members were perhaps responsible for compiling, writing, using, and preserving the Gospel of John.

A Brief Reader's Guide

One of the most well-known verses from the Bible is the one that begins the Gospel of John: "In the beginning was the Word, and the Word was with God, and the Word was God" (1:1). With this poetic flourish, the author of the Gospel simultaneously introduces the reader to a central argument about the identity of Jesus in the Gospel: Jesus, as "the Word," existed from the beginning of time. The author explicitly quotes from Genesis, identifies Jesus as the Word, the Logos, and places Jesus on par with God. "In the beginning" is an English translation for two Greek words: *en archē*. These words are exactly the same as those found in the Greek translation of the very first verse of the Bible, the first words of the Book of Genesis: "In the beginning (*en archē*) when God created the heavens and the earth" (Gn 1:1). The Fourth Gospel has used the Greek translation of the Old Testament, the Septuagint, and its quotation from Genesis is both deliberate and unmistakable. It works to make the claim that Jesus existed from the beginning of creation itself. And if there is any doubt about this for the reader, the Gospel continues in the second verse to clarify: "He was in the beginning with God" (Jn 1:2).

Let's look at these opening verses in context:

> In the beginning was the Word, and the Word was with God, and the Word was God.
>
> He was in the beginning with God. All things came into being through him, and without him not one thing came into being. What has come into being in him was life, and the life was the light of all people. The light shines in the darkness, and the darkness did not overcome it. (Jn 1:1–5)

Each Gospel signals its intent by how it begins, and the Gospel of John is no different. From the start, the reader finds a figure, the Word, who exists from the beginning of time, who had an important role in the creation of all things, and one who is equated with God. The term "Word" here is important. In Greek the word is *logos,* a term with a rich semantic range: it could mean a word spoken, an utterance, but it could also mean reason and law, a principle, a hypothesis or theory. In some classical Greek philosophical systems, the *logos* served as an intermediary, situated somewhere between the divine and human worlds. Here in John, the emphasis is on the preexistent nature of Jesus as the *logos.* The last verse of this opening signals one of John's key motifs: light and darkness. As we will see, this is just one of the many dualisms that animate the Fourth Gospel. It is both a literary and metaphorical device that gives rise to sharp distinctions.

The opening has long been viewed as a poetic prologue, possibly a poem or hymn, interrupted by brief narrative statements, such as: "There was a man sent from God, whose name was John. He came as a witness to testify to the light, so that all might believe through him. He himself was not the light, but he came to testify to the light. The true light, which enlightens everyone, was coming into the world" (Jn 1:6–9). In the space of just nine verses, the reader is taken from the presence of the Word at the beginning of all things to the figure of John the Baptist—not to be confused with John the disciple—who serves as a witness to "the light."

The prologue then shifts to the reception of "the light":

> He was in the world, and the world came into being through him; yet the world did not know him. He came to what was his own, and his own people did not accept him. But to all who received him, who believed in his name, he gave power to

> become children of God, who were born, not of blood or of the will of the flesh or of the will of man, but of God. (Jn 1:10–13)

Look at how the writer has now introduced a new character in these verses: the world, the cosmos. The Greek word *kosmos* was exceptionally rich in philosophical and political meaning: it could connote the order of things, the world order, the universe, or the earth, the world. The passage sets up a kind of tension between "the light"/"the Word" and the world. This tension will remain important throughout the Gospel. And there is another term in these verses that may at first not seem particularly unusual, but it is one that is significant for the subsequent use of John—the word "know" (in Greek, *ginōskō*). The idea that the world did not *know* "the Word" will become tremendously important to Christians in the second century who thought that knowledge was the key to salvation, as we will see. The Fourth Gospel is distinctive (especially in comparison to the Synoptic Gospels) in its repeated use of the language of *know* and *knowing*.

The prologue then concludes with the following:

> And the Word became flesh and lived among us, and we have seen his glory, the glory as of a father's only son, full of grace and truth . . . From his fullness we have all received, grace upon grace. The law indeed was given through Moses; grace and truth came through Jesus Christ. No one has ever seen God. It is God the only Son, who is close to the Father's heart, who has made him known. (Jn 1:14–18)

Here again, important terms and concepts are introduced to the reader: the idea that "the Word became flesh and lived among us" serves to bring the reader from the beginning of time to the present, and it transforms what might have seemed like an abstract "Word" into something fleshly, something tangible, an entity who has become human. And yet this is not just a human, for the grammatically challenging end to these verses implies that the Son is God. Of course, fundamental in these verses is the clarification that the Word that became flesh is Jesus Christ, and centuries after Jesus lived, this passage will become the linchpin of the Christian doctrine of the Incarnation. It's worth noting, too, that the writer also mentions the law given by Moses—the Torah, the Jewish Scriptures—in parallel to the grace and truth that came from Jesus Christ; over the course of the Gospel, as we will see, the writer does not regard them as exact parallels, but rather that the former is inferior to the latter.

The prologue of the Fourth Gospel serves as John's "birth" narrative, and this is how Christians long read the passage. Eventually, the first fourteen verses of John become the lectionary reading for Christmas Day, which commemorated Jesus's birth as early as the fourth century. It is useful here to introduce another term that will be important in subsequent chapters: Christology. When scholars speak about the Christology of a Gospel (or of any text) they are referring to its view of who Christ is/was. Put very simply: a high Christology refers to the idea that Christ is God; a low Christology refers to the idea of Christ as a human being. Christian doctrine will eventually, of course, claim that Jesus was both human and divine, but in the first century these ideas and the related ideas about a Trinity of Father, Son, and Holy Spirit were still rather fluid and undeveloped. The Fourth Gospel has been called "obsessively christological" by scholars such as Stephen Wilson, who sees Christology as "the overwhelmingly dominant theme in John."[2] In this opening, we certainly find high Christological ideas, as in "the Word is God," everything was created through the Word, and "the only Son" who seems to be identified as "God." But there is also the Word becoming flesh, which suggests that Jesus becomes human—a low Christology. Of course, these categories are not neat and tidy, but they are useful for identifying in broad strokes the various perspectives held by Christians about the figure of Jesus, and we will return to them in chapter 3.

After the prologue, the Fourth Gospel shifts to prose narrative. John the Baptist is questioned about his own identity by "the Jews" who "sent priests and Levites from Jerusalem" to question him. Is he the Messiah? The prophet Elijah? He responds, "I am not," and then he proceeds to quote from the prophet Isaiah: "I am the voice of one crying out in the wilderness, 'Make straight the way of the Lord'" (Jn 1:23). They continue to question John and he speaks about the "one who is coming." And then, "the next day he saw Jesus coming toward him and declared, 'Here is the Lamb of God who takes away the sin of the world'" (Jn 1:29). This identification of Jesus specifically as the "Lamb of God" is unique to the Gospel of John and only appears twice, here in verse 29 and again in verse 36. When the Greek text of John is translated into Latin a century or more later, this phrase becomes "Agnus Dei"; it eventually comes to form a key part of the Latin Mass and has a long rich history in subsequent liturgical traditions. The phrase "Lamb of God" in this Gospel serves as a shorthand for the idea that Jesus is the Passover sacrificial lamb, that he has taken the place of the lamb that was sacrificed as part of the Passover festival in early Judaism. These ideas are found in earlier Gospels, but John here clarifies Jesus's role beyond what we find elsewhere in the first century: Jesus is the lamb for all time, the one who takes away the sins of the world.

The remainder of this first chapter depicts Jesus gathering disciples, who call him by a variety of terms: "rabbi," which was a Hebrew and Aramaic word that simply meant "teacher";

"messiah," which again in Hebrew and Aramaic meant "anointed one"; "Jesus son of Joseph from Nazareth"; an "Israelite"; and, finally, "the Son of God" and "the "King of Israel." Look at this list of titles for Jesus: each of these shows Jesus's humanness. Although we might think "messiah" was a divine title, in Jesus's day, the term "messiah" could be used for kings who were anointed at their coronation or a mysterious figure who might play a role in ushering in a new age on earth. As John Ashton puts it: The messiah "is a man anointed by God and sent by him at the end of time to assist him in establishing his kingly rule."[3] "Son of God," too, was an old phrase that in the Jewish scriptures could refer to someone who had a special relationship with God or to a collective of those who were obedient to God. In its Greek context, this phrase could identify an individual as the child of a human mother and a Greek god. This is where neat distinctions between high and low Christology become much more complex. The list of disciples who follow Jesus here at the start of this Gospel, those who hear some of these titles for Jesus, include Andrew, Simon Peter (who is also explicitly called Cephas), Philip, and Nathanael.

As the narrative now continues, the writer turns to one of Jesus's miracles, the story of Jesus changing water into wine at a wedding in the village of Cana in Galilee. When a wedding party ran out of wine, Jesus tells the "servants" to "fill the jars with water"; when they then draw liquid from the jars and taste it, they find that it is "good wine." In his imaginative *A Life of Jesus,* the Japanese novelist Shusaku Endo described the story as "coming like a springtime zephyr between other events."[4] It's a story unique to this Gospel and we will return to it in later chapters, but I want to highlight here how the story ends: "Jesus did this, the first of his signs, in Cana of Galilee, and revealed his glory; and his disciples believed in him" (Jn 2:11). Much can be said about this single verse: first, Jesus's action, as I have already suggested, is called a "sign"—in Greek the word is *sēmeion*, a term that was used for a signal, such as a signal used to start a battle, or an omen, a signal about what was to come. A *sēmeion* was meant to be heard or seen; it was not a secret. And here in John's Gospel it points to who Jesus is and leads his disciples to "believe in him." So important is the theme of "signs" in the Fourth Gospel that some scholars have called the first half of the Gospel (Jn 1–12) "the Book of Signs," and they have suggested that it was initially a separate source.[5]

Immediately following the story of the wedding in Cana, Jesus goes up to Jerusalem (the first of three trips he makes to Jerusalem in this Gospel), where he finds "people selling cattle, sheep, and doves, and the money changers seated at their tables" (Jn 2:14). Using "a whip of cords," Jesus forces them out of the Temple, overturns the tables of the "money changers," and he tells them to "stop making my Father's house a marketplace!" (Jn 2:14–16). This story is found in the Synoptic Gospels, but always near the end, just before Jesus's arrest; indeed, in Matthew, Mark, and Luke it provides, in part, an explanation for his trial and execution. Its function here seems to be rather different, for it introduces the character of "the Jews" who question him about his actions in the Temple, to which he responds: "Destroy this temple, and in three days I will raise it up," a clear foreshadowing of his death and resurrection. It also serves as yet another sign (*sēmeion*) that leads "many" to believe in him (Jn 2:23). John's version of Jesus in the Temple is the only one to include the detail about the "whip of cords" and we will return to this image, because it takes on new significance during the medieval Crusades.

The next chapter contains the story of a Pharisee named Nicodemus, "a leader of the Jews," who questions Jesus about his claim that "no one can see the kingdom of God without being born from above" (Jn 3:3); Jesus's response to Nicodemus includes statements that will become some of the most widely memorized verses in Christian history, including:

> Very truly, I tell you, no one can enter the kingdom of God without being born of water and spirit. (Jn 3:5)
>
> Very truly, I tell you, we speak of what we know and testify to what we have seen. (Jn 3:11)
>
> No one has ascended into heaven except the one who descended from heaven, the Son of Man. . . . so must the Son of Man be lifted up, that whoever believes in him may have eternal life. (Jn 3:13–15)
>
> For God so loved the world that he gave his only Son, so that everyone who believes in him may not perish but may have eternal life. (Jn 3:16)

The last verse here is one that has long served as something of a creed for evangelical Christians, and we will return to it in chapter 6. We will also return to Nicodemus in chapter 5. For now, I want to highlight a few features in the story. First, the phrase "being born from above" is just one possible translation of a curious Greek passage. You might be more familiar with the translation "being born anew" or "being born again," perhaps the most widely used translation and, again, one that has become important to evangelicals.

One of the interesting things about the statements Jesus makes in the story of Nicodemus is its vertical imagery: "being born from above," "the one who descended from heaven," and the "Son of Man be lifted up." These phrases confirm one of the key themes in this Gospel—namely, that Christ descended to the earth from the heavens and will reascend to the heavens. We will see how this idea becomes important for later Christians, especially those with gnostic inclinations. According to Wayne Meeks, "the descent/ascent of Jesus seems to serve as the warrant for the esoteric revelation which he brings."[6] I also want to note that the phrase "Very truly" (also commonly rendered "Truly, truly") is a translation of a Greek phrase (*amēn, amēn*), which itself comes from Hebrew. It is where we get our English word "Amen."

Following the story of Nicodemus, the Fourth Gospel turns to stories of Jesus performing baptisms and a return to John the Baptist, who when questioned about a baptism for purification, speaks again about Jesus: "The one who comes from above is above all; the one who is of the earth belongs to the earth and speaks about earthly things. The one who comes from heaven is above all" (Jn 3:31). Again, we find here the language of heaven and earth, above and (implied) below, emphasized.

The story of Jesus and the Samaritan woman in John 4 is surely one of the iconic stories from the Fourth Gospel. Jesus sees a woman from Samaria about to draw water at the well, asks her for a drink, and then a conversation ensues between the two of them about thirst, water, and eternal life. Jesus surprises the woman by knowing about her past and she comes to believe he is a prophet at first. But the conversation then takes a turn: "Woman, believe me," Jesus says, "the hour is coming when you will worship the Father neither on this mountain nor in Jerusalem. You worship what you do not know; we worship what we know, for salvation is from the Jews" (Jn 4:21–22). His response should sound somewhat strange to us, for Samaritans shared Israelite ancestry with Jews, although they worshiped on Mount Gerizim rather than in the Temple of Jerusalem. But note, too, the repeated use of the word "know." It is fitting that the story concludes with the woman saying that she *knows* the Messiah is coming and Jesus responds: "I am he, the one who speaking to you." This is classic Johannine language: Jesus, throughout the Fourth Gospel, speaks with "I am" statements; some *know* who he is, but the majority do not.

The phrase "I am," used so frequently in the Gospel of John, is significant: in Greek, the words for "I am" are *egō eimi,* and they echo the story of Moses at the burning bush from the Book of Exodus. Here, God tells Moses to go to Pharoah to ask for the release of the enslaved Israelites in Egypt. God says to Moses, "*I am* the God of your father, the God of Abraham, the God of Isaac, and the God of Jacob" (Exodus 3: 6). When Moses asks what God's name is so that he can relay to the Israelites who has sent him, God says, "*I am who I am*" and "say to the Israelites '*I am* has sent me to you'" (Ex 3:14). In the Greek translation of the Hebrew text of Exodus, the words "I am" are rendered *egō eimi.* For the earliest readers of the Fourth Gospel, the allusion would have been unmistakable: Jesus is identifying himself in the same way that God did in Exodus as "I am." This is yet another distinctive feature of John that serves to elevate the divinity of Jesus.

After the story of the Samaritan woman, Jesus heals an official's son at Capernaum in Galilee, a healing that is called "the second sign that Jesus did after coming from Judea to Galilee" (Jn 4:54). And then he returns to Jerusalem to a pool where there were "blind, lame, and paralyzed" people lying. He tells one of them "stand up, take your mat and walk"—and the man is healed. This sparks fury among "the Jews," however, because it was the Sabbath, the day of rest. At this point in the Gospel we begin to see the collective character "the Jews" (in Greek, *hoi ioudaioi*) take an increasingly antagonistic stance against Jesus: "The Jews were seeking all the more to kill him" (Jn 5:18). But note that this comes very close on the heels of Jesus saying that "salvation is from the Jews" in his conversation with the Samaritan woman.

This is one of the intriguing, and often troubling, tensions in the Fourth Gospel—namely, its fraught stance toward Jews and Judaism. At the end of this story, Jesus launches into a lengthy speech about the truth of his testimony, the failure of some to believe him, and he claims: "If you believed Moses, you would believe me, for he wrote about me" (Jn 5:46).

The crowds continue to gather around Jesus and, back in Galilee, he performs the miracle of the loaves and fishes: from "five barley loaves and two fishes" Jesus feeds a multitude of five thousand, with plenty of food left over. This is one miracle that the Fourth Gospel shares with the Synoptic Gospels, but here it is called, again, a "sign" and it launches another speech about Jesus's identity: "I am the bread of life" (Jn 6:35); "I am the bread that came down from heaven" (Jn 6:41); "I am the living bread that came down from heaven. Whoever eats of this bread will live forever; and the bread that I will give for the life of the world is my flesh" (Jn 6:51). This troubles "the Jews," who think he is talking about his body being eaten (and his blood drunk), and it bothers even some of his disciples, who do not understand what he is saying. The narrative now becomes more tense, because "the Jews were looking for an opportunity to kill him" (Jn 7:1). When Jesus returns to Jerusalem, controversy follows him: "the Jews" question his authority, ask whether he is demon-possessed, and try to arrest him. All of this provides more opportunity for Jesus to speak about his identity.

What follows is the story of the woman "caught in the very act of committing adultery." We will spend substantial time later with this story, which was probably added to the Gospel after it was written; for now, I want simply to note its placement within a long section that describes opposition to Jesus—all of which allows him to claim his identity: "I am the light of the world," he says. "Whoever follows me will never walk in darkness but will have the light of life" (Jn 8:12). And: "I know where I have come from and where I am going, but you do not know where I come from or where I am going" (Jn 8:14); "You are from below, I am from above; you are of this world, I am not of this world" (Jn 8:23); "When you have lifted up the Son of Man, then you will realize that I am he" (Jn 8:28). In the way that the Fourth Gospel includes such statements, there is seemingly no mystery, no parables, yet "the Jews" become increasingly angry, and they debate with Jesus about Abraham, their ancestor. The tension crescendos until the point that Jesus says, "You are from your father the devil, and you choose to do your father's desires. He was a murderer from the beginning and does not stand in the truth, because there is no truth in him" (Jn 8:44). We will return to this striking passage, because it provides leverage for Christian antisemitism throughout history.

The tone of the narrative is now one of outright hostility. Jesus continues to perform healings and continues to be interrogated and opposed. After Jesus heals a blind man, "the Jews" and "some of the Pharisees" question the legitimacy of the healing. Was the man actually blind, they ask. The parents of the man tell them to ask him for themselves, "because they were afraid of the Jews; for the Jews had already agreed that anyone who confessed Jesus to be the Messiah would be put out of the synagogue" (Jn 9:22). This passage is both an indictment of "the Jews," but also may well reveal the dating of the Gospel itself, for we have no evidence that during Jesus's life that there was a ban on Jesus's followers attending synagogue. Rather, the first hint of a possible expulsion of Jesus followers from synagogues appears toward the end of the first century, though there continues to be much debate about the historicity of the available evidence on this point.

As strife mounts and calls for Jesus's execution continue, we find next in the Fourth Gospel Jesus's raising of Lazarus (11:1–44), Mary anointing Jesus's feet with perfume (Jn 12:1–8), Jesus heading back to Jerusalem and the crowds lining his path with palm branches (Jn 12:12–15), and Jesus washing the feet of his disciples (Jn 13:1–12). The story of the raising of Lazarus—a story unique to the Gospel of John—is particularly important for understanding how this Gospel depicts miracles; it is also a story with a rich afterlife in art, music, poetry, and even medicine. In the story, Mary and Martha, sisters of Lazarus, send word to Jesus saying that Lazarus was ill: "Lord, he whom you love is ill, they say" (Jn 11:3). What's odd, however, is that in spite of Jesus's love for Lazarus, he stays away: "Although Jesus loved Martha and her sister and Lazarus, after having heard that Lazarus was ill, he stayed two days longer in the place where he was" (Jn 11:6). The deliberate delay in going to Bethany serves a purpose here, for by the time Jesus arrives, Lazarus has already been buried for several days, and so Jesus's miracle is even more dramatic. Now he will not simply heal a sick person, he will raise Lazarus from the dead! First, he instructs Martha that "I am the resurrection and the life; those who believe in me, even though they die, will live, and everyone who lives and believes in me will never die" (Jn 11:25–26). As Jesus sees Mary weeping, he also weeps, in what is often considered the shortest verse in the Bible ("Jesus wept" or, more precisely, "Jesus began to weep," 11:35). He instructs those present at the tomb to roll the stone away, and then calls out to Lazarus: "Lazarus, come out!" Lazarus walks out of the tomb (Jn 11:43–44). This story has been so influential that doctors now call a spontaneous resuscitation—when a dead person's heart suddenly starts to beat again—the Lazarus Syndrome or Lazarus Heart.

In the wake of raising Lazarus, Jesus faces increasing opposition. "The Jews" go to the Pharisees and chief priests to express alarm at the "signs" Jesus is doing; and "from that day on they planned to put him to death" (11:52). Jesus becomes increasingly "troubled in spirit" that even his own disciples do not know who he is. He continues teaching his disciples: "I am the way, the truth, and the life. No one comes to the Father except through me" (14:6). When he is questioned by his disciple Philip, Jesus responds with a speech that extends from chapter 14 through the end of chapter 16. He speaks about his coming death, about his identity—"I am the true vine, and my Father is the vine grower" (Jn 15:1)—and he urges his followers to "love one another as I have loved you" (Jn 15:12). He says these things to his disciples as a warning that they will be persecuted, that "they will put you out of the synagogues," and that they will be killed.

Following these lengthy speeches, the Gospel concludes with the story of Jesus's betrayal and arrest, his hearings before Annas and Caiaphas the high priest and then his trial before the Roman procurator Pilate. Pilate's reluctance to execute Jesus is striking in this Gospel: "I find no case against him," he says to the "chief priests" and "the Jews" (Jn 18:8). But they continue to demand his crucifixion: "If you release this man," they say to Pilate, "You are no friend of the emperor. Everyone who claims to be a king sets himself against the emperor" (19:12). Finally, "he handed him over to them to be crucified" (19:16). As Jesus hangs from the cross, he looks down to see

> his mother, his mother's sister, Mary the wife of Clopas, and Mary Magdalene. When Jesus saw his mother and the disciple whom he loved standing beside her, he said to his mother, "Woman, here is your son." Then he said to the

> disciple, "Here is your mother." And from that hour the disciple took her into his own home. (19:25–27)

The appearance of the "disciple whom he loved" is unique to the Fourth Gospel. We will look closely at this figure known as the "beloved disciple," a figure that appears earlier in the Gospel, just after Jesus washes the feet of his disciples and tells them that one of them will betray him. He appears again as a witness to the empty tomb, and the same figure will reappear at the very end of the Gospel where he is credited with writing the Gospel. It's a mysterious figure, and one who has inspired rich and imaginative speculation.

The story of Mary Magdalene coming to the tomb and finding it empty, running to tell the disciples, and then Jesus's appearances to the disciples shares much with the Synoptic Gospels, but some details are more developed in John. In particular, Jesus's appearance to Mary is striking: she first thinks he is the gardener, and she asks him where Jesus's body has been taken, and then "Jesus said to her, 'Mary.' She turned and said to him in Hebrew, 'Rabbouni!' (which means Teacher)." Jesus then says, "Do not hold on to me, for I have not yet ascended to the Father. But go to my brothers and say to them, 'I am ascending to my Father and your Father, to my God and your God'" (20:16–18). The phrase "do not hold on to me" will eventually be translated into Latin as *noli me tangere,* and it will go on to find a rich and diverse afterlife in Christian art, Gregorian chant, poetry, the field of botany (for example, with plants that are called "touch-me-nots"), and even the US military, which has used the English translation of the phrase "Don't tread on me."

Mary does as Jesus asks and as the disciples are gathered together behind closed doors ("for fear of the Jews"), he appears to them (20:19). The disciple Thomas at first doubts that Jesus is real, but Jesus tells him: "Put your finger here and see my hands. Reach out your hand and put it in my side. Do not doubt but believe" (20:27). The story of "Doubting Thomas" is yet another distinctive feature of the Gospel of John, and subsequent interpretations of the story fixate on the idea of Thomas touching Jesus, even though the story in John never says Thomas actually did so. Today, visitors to Rome can find Thomas's finger among the relics on display at the Basilica of Santa Croce in Gerusalemme.[7] The story of Thomas as told in John serves to emphasize again Jesus's humanness—his very real fleshly existence—here post-resurrection. Afterward, Jesus "did many other signs in the presence of his disciples," and he goes finally to Galilee to appear again with his disciples as they are fishing. He offers Simon Peter a last instruction: "Feed my sheep," he says (21:17). The Gospel concludes with "the disciple who is testifying to these things and has written them, and we know that his testimony is true" (21:24). This is a statement of authentication, intended to persuade readers of the veracity of its contents; the source, according to this claim, is none other than an eyewitness who speaks the truth.

In the Fourth Gospel, we find a confident and assured Jesus, a figure who knows he has come down from heaven, convinced he has the authority of one who existed with God from the beginning of time, and a figure who is not afraid to speak over and over again about his own identity and the truth of his convictions. Much of this Gospel consists of Jesus speaking at length. The miracle stories are dramatic (e.g., raising Lazarus from the dead) and they are explicitly called "signs." The dualist language (e.g., light and dark, above and below, those who believe and the world that does not) and the hostility of "the Jews" courses throughout the text. And yet when we look closely at the Gospel, there are some questions that emerge: Where did the author get the material for these speeches? And what about the miracles that do not appear in any other Gospels? How do we explain Jesus saying to the Samaritan woman that salvation is from "the Jews" and then saying to "the Jews" that their father is the devil? How can the wedding in Cana be called "the first sign" and the healing of the official's son be called the "second sign" when in between these two passages he does other "signs"? How do we account for the fact that this Gospel shares material with the Synoptics, like the multiplication of the loaves and fishes, and yet also departs radically from them? These may seem like trivial questions, but they have vexed readers of this Gospel for a long time.

Sources and Composition

Some scholars, as I mentioned above, have sought to explain some of the literary problems in the Fourth Gospel by reconstructing the sources that the author may have used.[8] I should emphasize that these sources remain hypothetical: we do not have independent evidence for these sources. For those employing source criticism—the study of a given text's sources and their modification—the most widely held opinion is that the author of the Fourth Gospel had, at the very least, a "Signs Source" and a "Sayings Source." This would help to explain the problem of the first and second signs in between which Jesus does other signs. The author, for example, may have spliced the Signs Source into other material. So, too, a hypothetical Sayings Source, also sometimes called the Discourse Source, could explain how this author includes such lengthy speeches from Jesus—sometimes he speaks for several chapters! Were these sources written and have they been lost to history? Were they oral? It is impossible, in my view, to know. We simply cannot know if they existed in any form. Those who subscribe to source theories have also suggested that the prologue to the Gospel was a separate, preexisting source, and that the passion narrative drew upon yet other sources. It is not my goal here to argue for or against source criticism, but rather to point to the ways that John has been understood by some scholars of the New Testament as a kind of bricolage, a Gospel built from prior sources, perhaps some of which were written down.

A more urgent and important question is how to understand what appear to be conflicting views within this Gospel about Jews, Jewish history, and the figure of Jesus. On the one hand, Jesus is called "Rabbi" in this Gospel, a "teacher." A rabbi within first-century Judaism was a teacher of Jewish law, an interpreter of the Jewish scriptures. The term signals both Jesus's Jewishness and his humanness. On the other hand, Jesus places himself on par with God (e.g., "I and the Father are one"), causing a hostile rupture with "the Jews," for whom such a claim compromised devout monotheism. And this phrase itself—"the Jews" (*hoi ioudaioi*)—needs itself to be reckoned with, since it is so distinctive to the Fourth Gospel. We will return to "the Jews" in chapter 4, but it's worth noting here at the outset that the phrase appears over sixty-five times in the Gospel and although there are a few cases where "the Jews" seem neutral or even positive, in the vast majority of instances, "the Jews" are depicted in a negative light, and as increasingly hostile to Jesus and his followers. It is not an accident that the author in this Gospel uses "the Jews" rather than "the crowds" or the "Pharisees and Sadducees" that we find in the Synoptic Gospels. The author reveals a bias, a depiction of Jews that is highly charged, highly negative. In part, this could be this author's way to explain Jesus's death, but this does not seem a sufficient reason. After all, the Synoptic Gospels are also trying to explain how and why a figure who was supposed to be the messiah was executed in the manner reserved for the worst criminals, crucifixion. Here, I think we need to pair the portrayal of "the Jews" with the suggestion in the Gospel that those who believe in Jesus have been expelled from the Synagogues (Jn 9:22).

This brings us to a highly influential explanation for these challenges of sources and bias—namely, what has come to be called the Johannine community.

The So-Called Johannine Community

One of the most widely held views about the Fourth Gospel is that its final form reveals the history of a community—the so-called Johannine community—one that began among Jesus's first followers, developed and grew over the course of the first century, and experienced a rupture with Jewish synagogues. First proposed by the New Testament scholar J. Louis Martyn, it's an idea that was further developed by Raymond Brown, one of its strongest advocates: "The Gospel," Brown argues, "must be read on several levels, so that it tells us the story both of Jesus and of the community that believed in him."[9] Brown goes on to detail what he regards as four phases in the life of the community. In simplified form his reconstruction goes like this: the first phase was the community closest to the time of Jesus—his immediate Jewish followers and those who claimed to have witnessed his resurrection. This community largely consisted of Palestinian Jews who continued to pray and worship in the synagogues. Over time, Jews who were opposed to the Temple in Jerusalem, such as Samaritans, and some gentiles (non-Jews), began to join these Jewish followers of Jesus. The major historical event of the destruction of the Jewish Temple in Jerusalem by the Romans in 70 CE was a catalyst for increasing tensions among the believers. Tensions began to rise as followers developed different ideas about Jesus's identity given political events. Some followers continued to regard Jesus as the Jewish messiah; others began increasingly to view him as divine, as equal to God. This explains the references to the expulsion of Jesus followers from the synagogues in the Gospel itself. To monotheistic Jews, calling Jesus God was tantamount to polytheism. All of this took place, according to Brown, prior to the writing of the Gospel, perhaps "stretching from the mid 50s to the late 80s."[10]

The second phase, in Brown's reconstruction, "involved the life-situation of the Johannine community at the time the Gospel was written."[11] The community now recalls the trauma of their expulsion from the synagogues and develops, in response, an ever-higher Christology and they begin to regard themselves in opposition to Judaism. Sociologists call this kind of development in response to trauma a "fortress mentality," whereby those who feel themselves to be persecuted build a sense of strict boundaries that establish stark divides between "us" and "them." Brown sees this phase as the time the Gospel was written in the 90s CE.

Brown goes further than the Gospel, however, and turns next to the Johannine Epistles. I mention this briefly here because it is important for understanding the idea of the Johannine community, even though 1, 2, and 3 John are beyond the scope of this book. In phase three, again according to Brown, division happens within the Johannine community—namely, divisions over Christological ideas. 1 John is a letter written to a community in schism: "They went out from us," the author writes, "but they did not belong to us; for if they had belonged to us, they would have remained with us" (1 Jn 2:19). This letter (and 2 and 3 John) suggests that those who had left the community held a Christology that was so high that they no longer regarded Jesus to be human. In response, the letter-writer emphasizes the truth of the community that has remained: "That which was from the beginning, which we have heard, which we have seen with our eyes, which we have looked upon and touched with our hands, concerning the word of life—this life was revealed, and we have seen it and testify to it, and declare to you the eternal life that was with the Father and was revealed to us" (1 Jn 1:1–2). The text surely does suggest schism, though it is difficult to establish precisely when, why, and where the schism happened. Brown suggests that it happens around 100 CE. And finally, during the last phase in the early second century, according to Brown, a multiplicity of divergent Christological views circulated among Christians in the eastern Mediterranean.

Brown's reconstruction of the Johannine community has been highly influential, but we need to remember that it is a reconstruction on the basis of existing evidence, which largely consists of the text of the Gospel and the Epistles themselves. There is little external evidence to support his ideas, although it's possible that a passage from rabbinic literature that mentions rejecting heretics in synagogues may have referred to these Jesus followers. The issue here is historically tenuous and arguments of this kind are frequently circular. More recently, the whole idea of a Johannine community has been questioned, especially by scholars such as Hugo Méndez, who regard the Gospel and the letters as "unreliable bases for historical reconstruction."[12] Although we do not need to go further into the weeds of scholarly debate, it is worth emphasizing that reconstructing the past is complex and in the case of the Johannine community we are dependent upon the Gospel itself. But even if we cannot securely reconstruct the life of a community, we still need to contend with two contexts: the context of Jesus's life and the context in which the Gospel was written.

Conclusion

For our purposes it is useful to reflect on the problems the Gospel poses for our understanding of Christianity's origins in the first century—and the uncertainty that surrounds the date, location, and author of the Gospel compounds these problems. There is much we still do not know. I find it intriguing to imagine the people behind the text of the Gospels, especially given how little we know beyond the Gospels and the writings of Paul about the earliest stages of what will eventually become known as Christianity. Yet we are hard pressed to know where the Fourth Gospel was written, even though some have suggested Ephesus in Asia Minor; when it was written, though scholars agree that it was written after the destruction of the Jerusalem Temple in 70 CE and most think it was written in the last decade of the first century; and of course, the most difficult question of all is the question of authorship. We will return to the character of the "beloved disciple" and his possible role in the writing of the Gospel, but the identity of the "beloved disciple" remains unclear. Subsequent Christian tradition notwithstanding—in particular, the Christian view that the "beloved disciple" was John, the son of Zebedee, the author of the Gospel—there is so much that we simply do not know.

2

"Word Made Flesh"

ENCOUNTERING THE FOURTH GOSPEL AS A BOOK

THE GOSPEL of John ends with a remarkable final flourish, one that identifies the (still unnamed) disciple responsible for writing the Gospel, and an acknowledgment that there are far more stories about Jesus than those found in this one Gospel:

> This is the disciple who is testifying to these things and has written them, and we know that his testimony is true. But there are also many other things that Jesus did; if every one of them were written down, I suppose that the world itself could not contain the books that would be written. (Jn 21:24–25)

A testimony. In Greek, the word here is *martyria,* which referred to a true testimony offered by a witness, *a martys,* from which we derive our word "martyr." But the author also reveals an awareness of many other stories, many that were not included in this one Gospel. Indeed, the narrator imagines that writing down all of the things that Jesus did would overfill the world with books. The passage is itself a witness to the importance attached to the act of writing and the creation of books; the word used for "books" here is *biblia* in Greek, from which we get our word "Bible." When Muslims call Christians and Jews "people of the book" some six centuries later, they do so with a keen sense of just how fundamental books were to these traditions.

It has become commonplace to think of the Bible as a physical book: reams of pages, written on both sides, bound along the spine—a book that can be opened, flipped through, read and reread. But early Christians had a complicated relationship to books. Christians inherited from their Jewish origins a reverence for the written word, the scriptures. In the first century, Jewish religious life centered on the annual festivals like Passover, the prayers and services in synagogues, religious observances in homes, and until 70 CE, the sacrificial rituals taking place in the Temple in Jerusalem. But the sacred scriptures held tremendous importance; indeed, they were authoritative sources for religious practice that eventually were accompanied by vast rabbinic literatures that interpreted them. The scriptures were essential to worship. When Jews went to synagogues to read from the scriptures, or to hear them read, though, they did not read from a book as we commonly think of books. Their scriptures were written in scroll form, long rolls that could be rolled up on one end as the other end was unrolled. The form of their rolls of scripture was similar to the scrolls of literature used by Greeks and Romans, although the status accorded them as sacred was altogether different. Rolls could be written on papyrus, a plant grown along the Nile in Egypt, or on parchment, sheets made from the skins of animals, such as goats. So, when the Gospel of John near its very beginning speaks of the "Word made flesh"—a phrase, as we have seen, that provides a prooftext for later doctrines about the Incarnation—we can also think of this as the written word transcribed onto skins prepared for writing. The word made flesh.

As the Christian movement began to expand over the course of the first and second centuries, Jewish scriptural consciousness continued among the earliest Christian congregations. The second-century Christian writer from what is now the city of Nablus in the West Bank, Justin Martyr, describes Christian worship in his day like this:

> And on the day called Sunday, all who live in cities or in the country gather together to one place, and the memoirs of the apostles or the writings of the prophets are read, as long as time permits. (*Apology* 1.67)

Justin here provides a window into the early Christian practice of reading from the Gospels and the prophets, by which he means books like Isaiah or Jeremiah. What made these scriptures so important? They told about the past, made meaning of the present, and spoke to the future. As the biblical scholar James Kugel writes, "The past was everywhere. It was what explained the present and was the standard by which the present was to be judged and upon which future hopes were to be based; and it was legitimacy."[1] Most Christians would have encountered the Gospel of John through hearing it read in worship, as Justin suggests, rather than by reading it privately. They would have heard stories from the Gospel circulating by word of mouth, one person to another recounting, say, the story of Lazarus or Nicodemus. This point is worth emphasizing: just because scripture was at the heart of the religious practice for both Jews and Christians, did not mean that everyone handled or even encountered these books, much less that most people could read them. Literacy rates were very low throughout antiquity. Some estimates put literacy at about 10 percent of the population, although these rates may have been somewhat higher among Jews.[2] And Christians, even after the Gospels and the letters of Paul were written, continued to value oral traditions. The fourth-century Christian historian, Eusebius of Caesarea, quotes from a second-century Christian writer named Papias, who explains why he privileges the oral testimony of eyewitnesses: "For I did not think," he says, "that information from the books would profit me as much as information from a living and surviving voice" (*Ecclesiastical History* 3.39).

The Ancient Book Trade

In early Christianity there was a decided ambivalence about books—an ambivalence that may be partly due to the nature of the ancient book trade itself. There were no ancient book publishers in the way that we think of them today: a publisher who publishes hundreds or thousands copies of a book, all identical to one another thanks to the use of both printing presses and technologies for mass production. In antiquity, no such mechanisms existed. Throughout the ancient world—and, indeed, all the way until the invention of the printing press in the fifteenth century—books were written and copied by hand. The term "manuscript" fittingly describes all of these books, since the word comes from two Latin words that mean "hand" (*manu*) and "to write" (*scriptus*).

So, let's say you were an ancient reader and you hoped to get your hands on a copy of the Gospel of John. How would you do it? Well, we have ancient letters that give us insight into one mechanism: "Make and send me copies of . . ." is how one reader wrote to another around the year 170 CE.[3] In this case, an individual was writing to a friend or an acquaintance asking them to make copies of a couple of books and to send them. That is one way in which books circulated in antiquity: person to person through social networks. Christian books also circulated among congregations. An individual in one congregation might prepare a copy for another; or a traveler going to a new congregation might bring along a copy of a book. In cities there were bookshops, but these, too, obtained their copies of books for sale through social networks and, above all, only with the work of scribes.

The whole process of book writing, copying, and disseminating texts of any kind depended on the work of scribes, who most frequently were employed to do the actual copying. Scribes were not a special class of society by the time Christianity emerges; they were sometimes slaves or freedpersons who were employed by a wealthy book lover or by a bookshop; but in other cases, they were individuals who had had enough education and training that they could make a copy for their own use. The vast majority of scribes were employed writing documents, drawing up petitions, keeping records, writing letters for those who were illiterate—in other words, they were employed in a wide variety of administrative tasks. The making of literary copies for individuals, libraries, bookshops, or (in the case of Christianity) for congregations was a small fraction of what we might think of as the culture of writing in antiquity.

There are important implications for our study of the Fourth Gospel that every book was handmade, hand copied, hand bound, and hand distributed in antiquity. The Gospel of John in its earliest form may well have been drafted by a particular individual, who may have regarded themselves as part author and part editor, but we do not have any original copy of the Gospel of John. No signed copy or original copies exist for any New Testament text. This is significant, because handwritten copies resulted in *variation*: no two copies of any text were identical. All kinds of changes crept into what we call the manuscript traditions: simple errors that scribes made, spelling mistakes, dropping words or lines, transposing words, and so forth. But scribes also sometimes deliberately made changes to their copies; when they read something in their exemplar that they considered erroneous or in need of correction, they sometimes made intentional changes to their copies.[4] We should expect, therefore, that the form of the Gospel of John varied over time and from place to place; we should expect that the copies of the Gospel of John that were circulating were not identical in terms of the words themselves. Variation was inevitable and we will look closely at this issue in the next chapter.

In this chapter, our attention is on the Gospel of John as a book. We can learn something about ancient readers of the Fourth Gospel by looking at the earliest manuscripts that remain. There are thousands of manuscripts of the Gospel of John, stretching from the second century through the medieval period, up to the invention of the printing press and well beyond. And even a brief survey of the manuscripts of John takes us into the world of translation, because already in the late second century, Christians began translating John from its original Greek into Latin and Syriac, and soon after, into Coptic, and later into Armenian, Arabic, and many other languages. Our primary focus here will be to get a sense of what it was like for an early Christian to encounter the Fourth Gospel as a book, beginning with the earliest remaining copies of John. What follows is a mere sample. Consider this a tour of some highlights of the early history of the Gospel of John on papyrus and parchment.

The Earliest Copies on Papyrus

The earliest copy we have of the Greek Gospel of John is a small papyrus fragment about the size of a credit card or an old flip phone. Because of its importance for understanding the history of the Fourth Gospel, whole books have been written on the tiny fragment. Now housed in the John Rylands Research Institute and Library at the University of Manchester in England, it was purchased in Egypt by a British scholar named Bernard Grenfell in 1920. Given its dry climate, which allows for the preservation of papyrus texts, Egypt is the origin of all our earliest remaining copies of texts that will eventually be included in the New Testament. The fragment has long been dated—through a study of its handwriting—to the first half of the second century, making it one of the earliest, if not *the* earliest, copy we have of any book contained in the New Testament. If we date the Gospel of John to roughly 95 CE, this fragment—written perhaps as early as 125 CE in Egypt—tells us that the Gospel was in circulation some thirty years later around the Mediterranean.[5]

The fragment contains portions of John 18:31–33 and 37–38. Let's look closely at some of the important features of the fragment. The first thing to notice is that it is written on both sides: the front (the recto) contains parts of verses 31–33; the back side (the verso) contains 37–38. Though it may seem unsurprising to find writing on both sides of the fragment, the fact is that in the ancient world most literary books were written on scrolls and these were inscribed only on one side. So, the writing on

FIGURE 2.1. *P. Ryl.* 457 (P^{52}); John 18:31–33, 37–38. Credit: The John Rylands Research Institute and Library, the University of Manchester.

the two sides suggests quite clearly that the fragment comes from a codex, not a roll. A codex is the ancestor of what we now call a book: a set of pages, inscribed on both sides and bound along one edge. Scholars have long looked to this fragment to suggest that from the outset, Christians seemed to have a preference for the codex format, possibly for the ease of cross-referencing, possibly for economical efficiency (after all, papyrus was expensive and writing on both sides was a better use of the resource), or perhaps because codices (especially small ones) were easier to hide in one's clothing and this might have been especially important during times of persecution. Another explanation that has often been given for the Christian use of codices is that this format served to distinguish their books from both Jewish biblical scrolls as well as Greek and Roman literature.

We can reconstruct the size of the Rylands codex by calculating its dimensions on the basis of what remains: it would have been roughly 8 inches by 8 inches and had about 130 pages (leaves), a small square book that could be easily carried or used for private reading. Think about holding such a book in your hands: it's small enough to be manageable, and it can be transported and perhaps hidden in your clothing; you might read it privately, but it could also be used to read aloud in a congregation.

Another feature we find even in this small fragment is one shared by other literary texts from the same time period: there are no word divisions; rather, the text runs continuously without wordbreaks. There were also few punctuation marks and no paragraph or chapter and verse organization that we have come to take for granted with our contemporary Bibles. What this means is that those who read this copy of the Gospel of John were probably already familiar with the text. The study of handwriting in manuscripts is a field unto itself—namely, palaeography, which can tell us about both the copyist and the users of the codex. The handwriting in this fragment has been called "informal," "practiced," and "workaday."[6] It is not the handwriting we would expect to find, say, in a professional copy of Homer at the time. Here is a scribe who may have been trained to write administrative documents—like petitions, contracts, or letters—who has undertaken to copy the Gospel of John perhaps for private use. Of course, this must remain a tentative conclusion, because there is no colophon, a note identifying the scribe that was sometimes affixed to the end of a manuscript.

Let's look at one more early papyrus copy of the Gospel of John—one that contains the whole Gospel, although some leaves have degraded and most of chapter 21 is missing. This codex also comes from Egypt and is now housed in the Bodmer Library in Geneva, Switzerland. It is even smaller than the

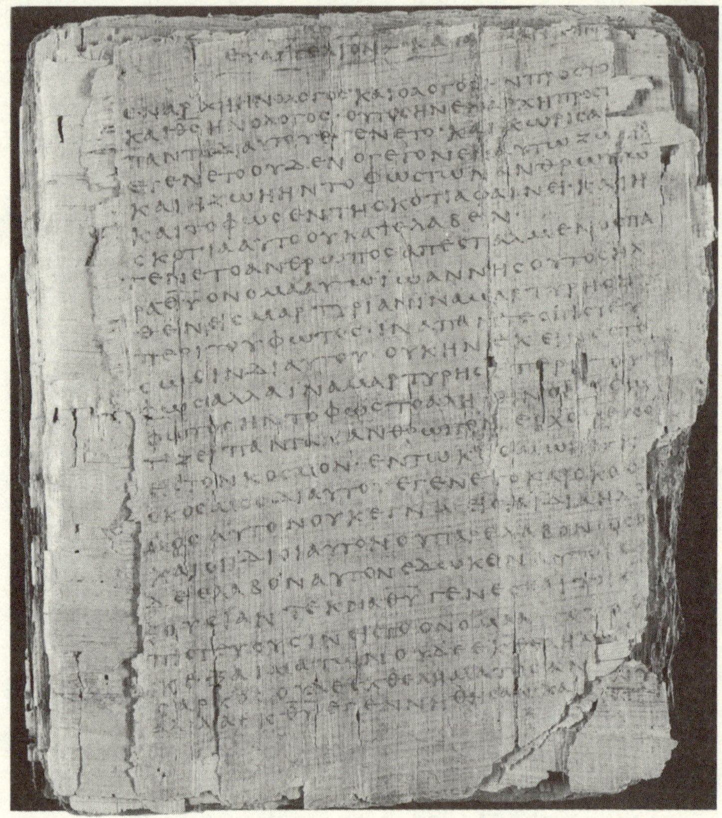

FIGURE 2.2. *Papyrus Bodmer* 2 (P^{66}), Bibliotheca Bodmeriana. Credit: Fondation Martin Bodmer, Geneva.

Rylands codex would have been; the pages are roughly 6.5 inches by 5.5 inches—almost a miniature book. We cannot precisely date this codex, though palaeographic analysis suggests a date around 200 CE. As with the Rylands fragment, there are no word divisions, the handwriting is skilled but not necessarily professional, it is in codex format, and it is roughly square. One of the remarkable things about this codex is that so much of it is intact: it allows us to read almost the entire Gospel of John in a book written some 1,800 years ago.

We discover, too, an important feature of the ancient copies of the New Testament texts in this codex: often, there was more than one scribe involved in making a copy. Here is one of the things we can trace in a close examination of this codex: the relationship between the writing of the text and the editing of it. Throughout the codex, there are corrections made, either by the original scribe or by another one. For a long time scholars thought that the many corrections in this Bodmer codex suggested a lazy scribe or one who was not well trained, perhaps a Christian who had just enough writing skills to be able to make a copy, but not a skilled professional. But if we look closely at a single page, we can see that the writing is actually quite even and consistent; it is a hand that has had a lot of practice, and the appearance of corrections, sometimes perhaps by a different scribe, actually suggests that a lot of care was put into making this an accurate copy. The care taken to correct suggests that the book mattered to those who copied and used it.

One other important feature is worth emphasizing: the text of the Gospel of John filled the codex. We no longer have the covers of the codex, but we can read John 1:1 on the very first page. Above the beginning, at the very top of the first leaf, we see a title; what remains allows us to read "Gospel according to John" (*euaggelion kata Iōannēn*). The physical features of this copy teach us how Christian texts, including the Gospel of John, would have circulated in the earliest period: not necessarily bound with other Gospels or with letters of Paul, but on their own. It is very likely that in the second century and perhaps well into the third, a congregation might only have a copy of one Gospel. Even though the quality of the papyrus in this codex is not particularly good, suggesting a lower cost, books were still rather expensive. And the book technology necessary for making a large codex—big enough to fit, say, four Gospels—did not yet exist in the second century. So when Irenaeus, writing in the second century, complains that some Christians seem to draw their heretical ideas from one particular Gospel, and other heretics look to a different one, it's important to remember that it is entirely possible, even likely, that a congregation in the second century may have had only one Gospel, and that this one Gospel informed their Christological and theological views. This point will become especially important for us in the next chapter.

Christian Biblical Codices

The earliest Christian Bible with Old and New Testaments that has survived is the so-called Codex Sinaiticus, dated to the mid-fourth century. To understand the significance of this codex, it is important to put it into historical context: in the early fourth century, the Roman Emperor Constantine converted to Christianity, though there continues to be debate about the extent of his conversion or whether we should even call it a conversion. This development dramatically shaped the subsequent history of Christianity, and we will return to it in the next chapter. One of the tangible impacts of Constantine's so-called conversion was on the history of the Christian Bible. Within just a few short decades, the social and economic demographics of Christianity began to shift as wealthy elites began converting to Christianity in ever greater numbers and they invested in building Christian churches and monasteries—monasteries where groups of monks could be trained as scribes. The effect on the production of Christian Bibles was striking: now multiple copies could be made at the same time with a scriptorium full of scribes who made copies as a reader read the text aloud. These scribes were making copies by dictation, not necessarily by looking at an exemplar and then trying to copy it. The material on which books were copied also shifted from papyrus—whose origin was Egypt, and which was not well protected against decay and rot—to parchment and, in particular, a kind of expensive high-quality parchment called vellum.

Vellum codices changed the course of book history, because vellum—as a material—could be used for much larger codices. Christians could now produce Bibles with Old and New Testaments bound together. Codex Sinaiticus is one of these. Made in the fourth century CE, it is named after the place it was found—namely, the Monastery of Saint Catherine's in Sinai, an important region for the development of Christian monasticism.[7] The contents of the codex today include roughly 400 pages that contain about half of the Old Testament and all of the New Testament, including several texts not found today in the New Testament. The book is impressive in size: 15 by 13.5 inches for each page, which meant that when it was opened, it would have been over two feet wide. This would have been a book meant for public recitation and it would have required the use of a lectern. To produce a codex like this was expensive, time-consuming, and labor intensive.

In recent years, the whole codex has been digitized and is now readily available for viewing online.[8] Even an untrained eye can see just how different the material and handwriting are from the papyrus books we looked at above. The handwriting is highly skilled, with each letter inscribed with painstaking care on the fine vellum. The process would have been extremely slow even though multiple scribes served as copyists. Instead of one column of text, there are now four even columns on each page. In addition, the manuscript does not have word divisions, but it marks off paragraphs and in the margins of the columns there are letters and numbers that formed a liturgical reading guide. We can also see many places where an editor (or sometimes the original scribe) has come along to make corrections—to change, add, or delete words written by previous scribes.

Other fourth- and fifth-century codices of the Christian Bible have survived. Some are now housed at the Vatican in Rome; others at the Freer Gallery of Art in Washington, DC; the British Library in London; and elsewhere. Taken collectively, they are important for book history broadly speaking as well as the history of Christianity. For our understanding of the Gospel of John, they reveal how the Gospel of John comes to be bound in a codex with the Synoptic Gospels, thereby allowing for easier comparison between Gospel stories. The implications of what may seem inconsequential are important, for binding the four Gospels of Matthew, Mark, Luke, and John together ensures that they are read as a collection, which obscures the distinctions between the Gospels. One Gospel cannot be read on its own. A codex like Sinaiticus would have inspired awe among those who handled and read it, and by those who encountered it perhaps in the context of a congregational reading. Over time, Christian Bibles become more and more elaborate and ornate, some filled with colorful illuminations, others bound by jewel-embedded covers.[9]

Early Versions of the Gospel of John

Thus far, I have been focused on the earliest copies of the Gospel of John in its original Greek. But by the late second century we already find the Gospel being translated into Latin and Syriac, the languages of early Christians in the western Mediterranean and Syria, respectively. A couple of centuries later, Christians in Egypt began translating the Greek

New Testament into Coptic, the latest stage of the Egyptian language. The New Testament was subsequently translated into Armenian, Ethiopic, Gothic, and many other languages.[10] Each one of these versions was made in response to the expansion of Christianity into new regions, as Greek ceased to be the lingua franca—the common language—of the Mediterranean world. One of the fascinating ways that Christians began to produce versions was to prepare bilingual manuscripts. Perhaps the most important of these is Codex Bezae, a bilingual Greek and Latin codex with Greek on the left side page and Latin on the right, dating to the fifth century. It is a striking codex and one that has been studied extensively. For the history of the Gospel of John, one of the (many) unusual features of this codex is that it is the "oldest manuscript to contain the story of the adulterous woman (John 7:53–8:11)," a story that is found only in the Gospel of John and one we will return to, for it has an interesting history all its own.[11]

Codex Bezae is helpful for understanding how the translation of the Fourth Gospel developed in late antiquity, and it is especially important for the transition in the West to Latin as the primary language of scripture. Latin manuscripts of the Fourth Gospel, and of the New Testament more generally, began to proliferate in the fourth century and later; some included beautiful illuminations (paintings) and highly stylized scripts. One especially striking Latin manuscript of the Gospels is what is known as the Lindisfarne Gospels, produced in the eighth century and used at the Island of Lindisfarne, just off the coast of northwest England and now housed in the British Museum in London.[12] Lindisfarne was an important center of monastic Christianity as it moved into western Europe and the British Isles. The Lindisfarne Gospels are written in an elaborate and ornate style, employing skills of multiple kinds; it was expensive and time-consuming to produce, and it is almost certainly the work of a monastery.

We can look to other early versions to help us understand the transmission of the Gospel of John its earliest centuries. One fascinating example of Christian book culture is that of a codex called Syriac Sinaiticus, which is a 4th–5th century codex of the Gospels in Syriac, the language of Christians in the eastern Mediterranean. It is called "Sinaiticus," because like Codex Sinaiticus above, it was found at St. Catherine's Monastery in Sinai. But here is what is especially fascinating about this codex: the Syriac text of the Gospels inscribed on the codex was at some point rubbed out (i.e., erased) and then Syriac stories of holy women were written on top. With modern technology we can read the underlayer, so we are able to use the codex to understand more about Syriac versions of the Gospels. The fact that this codex contains an underlying text that had been erased so that a new text could be inscribed in the codex makes this codex what we call a palimpsest, a book where the first inscribed text has been rubbed out (or partially erased) in order to inscribe something new on top. A palimpsest literally translated from Greek means "to write again."

Any claim that early Christians viewed their scriptures, including the Gospel of John, as sacred and inviolable needs to account for examples like Syriac Sinaiticus and to explain why a copy of John's Gospel was erased so that the story of a Christian woman could be written instead. We also need to account for the fact that so many of our earliest copies of the Gospel of John were found on ancient trash heaps. Were they worn out or damaged from use? Were they no longer relevant? Had other texts become more important? It's not always easy to know.

Christian Amulets

Before leaving the topic of the Gospel of John as a book, I want to highlight another way that Christians encountered the Fourth Gospel in physical written form. We often think that there is a stark distinction to be made between magic and religion, but one of the interesting things to observe about the earliest forms of John as a text is to find amulets or charms that contained passages from the Gospel of John (as well as other Gospels). One especially well-preserved example is a fifth-century long and narrow—some nine inches long and just under two inches wide—papyrus sheet on which the opening to John's Gospel is written. Found in the archaeological remains of the Egyptian village of Oxyrhynchus, the papyrus was first published in 1911; more recently, it has received renewed interest for the details it provides about how Christian women, in particular, may have sometimes used biblical texts.[13]

The text begins as follows:

> Flee, hateful spirit, Christ drives you out. The Son of God and the Holy Spirit have gained advantage over you. God of the sheep-pool, rescue Joannia, to whom Anastasia also called Euphemia gave birth, from every evil. In the beginning was the word, and the word was with God and God was the word. All things came into being by him and without him not anything came into being that has come into being.

Notice how this amulet begins with a curse or warning against the "hateful spirit," and calls on the authority of Christ, the Son of God, and the Holy Spirit. In the third sentence, we find the quotation of John 1:1, 3. After the quotation, the text returns to what seems like either a prayer or a plea for protection:

> Lord Christ, son and word of the living God, the one who healed every disease and every sickness, heal and look upon your female slave Joannia . . . and expel from her and put to flight every fever . . . on account of the prayers and entreaties of our mistress, the God-bearer, and of the glorious archangels and of John, the holy and glorious apostle and evangelist and theologian.

Look at the multiple ways this amulet engages with the Gospel of John. First, one wonders whether it is a coincidence that John is quoted in an amulet for Joannia; her name (*Iōannia*) is the feminine version of the name John (*Iōannēn*). The Gospel of John is quoted directly. And finally, the prayers of Mary, the archangels, and the evangelist John are invoked. Given all of these features, as well as the fact that it was found in Oxyrhynchus, a city with the only known sanctuary dedicated to John at this time, AnneMarie Luijendijk has written that it is clear "the composer of our amulet had a special affinity with the fourth evangelist."[14]

Given the shape (long and narrow) and contents (scripture and prayers for healing) of this text, we can be fairly certain that this was an amulet, designed to be rolled up and worn around someone's neck or hung by someone's bedside as a kind of talisman or charm intended to ward off evil. This one was made to heal a certain Joannia, and to ward off future illnesses. Although the practice of wearing an amulet like this might seem to be akin to magic, we know about devout Christians who wore amulets from writers like John Chrysostom and Jerome. In a fourth-century sermon, for example, Chrysostom urges his congregants to "scorn those who want to chant over you an incantation or tie an amulet to your body" (*Homilies Against Judaizing Christians* 7.1). These writers were concerned about the practice, but they also provide clear evidence that it was indeed a Christian practice—how widespread we cannot know. We have dozens of such amulets, some written on papyrus sheets, others inscribed in pieces of wood or ceramic. Many of them contain brief stories of Jesus performing healings or passages from the Lord's Prayer. They expand our understanding of what it meant to encounter the Fourth Gospel in physical and textual form.

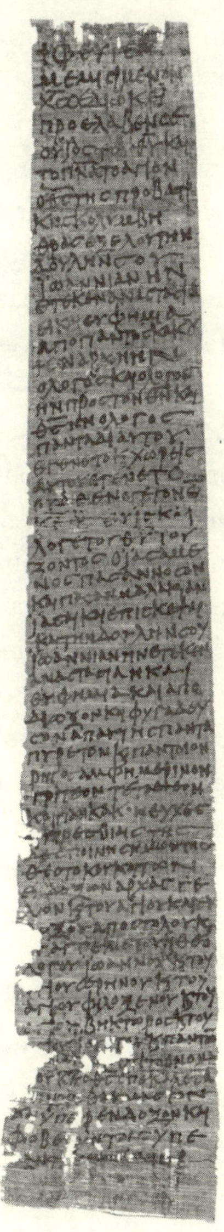

FIGURE 2.3. Amulet. MS Gen 1026, *Oxyrhynchus Papyrus* 1151. Credit: Courtesy of University of Glasgow Archives & Special Collections.

The Fourth Gospel in Early Christian Art

Until now, I have focused on how early Christians would have encountered the Fourth Gospel as a book or as an amulet—both of which reveal something about how the text itself came to be inscribed and translated in written form. But there is another way that Christians encountered the Gospel, and that is through the visual medium of art. The earliest Christian art comes from funerary contexts, with the catacombs in Rome providing some of our very earliest examples. The history of early Christian art is beyond our scope, but I want to highlight the unique role that the Gospel of John plays from a very early stage. According to the art historian

Robin Jensen, "images from the Gospel of John account for about half of all the New Testament scenes in third- and fourth-century Christian art."[15] The story of the raising of Lazarus or Jesus changing water into wine at Cana, Jesus with the Samaritan woman at the well or Jesus healing the blind man—all of these stories appear with some frequency, suggesting at the very least that the stories from the Fourth Gospel held particular fascination. These were stories that warranted illustration—painted in tombs, carved into stone sarcophagi, engraved on wooden panels, molded on clay oil lamps, or constructed of elaborate tile mosaics. When we remember that the world in which the Fourth Gospel first circulated was primarily an oral one and that storytelling was essential to the spread of Christianity, it should come as no surprise that the dramatic stories of miracles in John's Gospel were especially ripe for artistic renderings.

For now, we can look at one example as illustrative. The very earliest identifiably Christian art derives primarily from the catacombs in Rome, a set of underground corridors containing tombs or burials. Throughout the catacombs, which may have been used as places for Christians to gather during times of persecution, we find rooms with paintings of Gospel scenes. One example is the story of Lazarus from the Fourth Gospel painted in the Catacomb of Callixtus in the third century. The image is striking in its simplicity: the figure Jesus stands on the right with his hand gesturing toward a tomb, here depicted as an above-ground mausoleum, with a figure (Lazarus) standing in front of the open doorway. In his left hand, Jesus appears to hold a pointer or wand, though it gestures away from the tomb. The frequency with which we find the story of Lazarus depicted is telling: it is not just that it is a dramatic miracle story but also that it serves in subsequent interpretation,

FIGURE 2.4. "The Raising of Lazarus," Catacomb of Callixtus. Credit: Josef Wilpert.

as Jensen argues, to prove "that God can bring the dead back to life, either here or in paradise."[16]

Words were not needed to explain the image or the story—viewers would have recognized this immediately as the story of Jesus's raising of Lazarus. The basic visual features of a figure emerging from a tomb, sometimes wrapped in cloth, and a Jesus facing the tomb will come to be echoed in countless later artistic renderings of the story of Lazarus. Each of these representations of the story shares the same basic features, but they are reimagined in their contemporary context. Mosaics in imperial basilicas will, for example, depict Jesus wearing royal robes; medieval paintings show John, with a monk's tonsure, standing with Mary and Martha beside Jesus; in the modern world, an art project in Cameroon called JESUS MAFA, shows a Jesus clad in red robes and standing alongside Mary, Martha, and joyous children as he gestures toward a Lazarus emerging from a cave-tomb. In all of these instances, visual representations reveal that Christians throughout history have encountered the Fourth Gospel well beyond its form as a book. Indeed, if we look at how the story of Lazarus has made its way into music (e.g., David Bowie's song "Lazarus"; Sting's "The Lazarus Heart"; Dave Van Ronk's "Poor Lazarus"; Aretha Franklin's "Mary, Don't You Weep"), films (e.g., R. L. Scott's 2021 film *Lazarus*), and poetry (e.g., Paul Mariani's "Pietà"), we find that the stories from the Gospel of John have found rich afterlives far exceeding their placement in a book.[17]

Conclusion

We will return to the varied afterlives of Johannine stories. My goal in this chapter has been more modest: to trace the early history of the Gospel of John as a book. From the earliest centuries, Christians would certainly have heard passages read from the Gospel in church services, they would have told and retold stories from the Gospel, and they would have seen images from the Gospel painted on walls, carved into marble panels, and built from mosaics on basilica ceilings. Our primary focus has been on the physical form of the Gospel as a book in its earliest centuries—the material residue of the earliest legacy of the Gospel of John. The "word made flesh" literally came to resonate with the written words on the flesh/skins of animals, on parchment and vellum. Along the way, Christians played an influential role in book history: their adoption of the codex form, instead of the roll, was to have enormous influence. The tiny fragment of the Fourth Gospel found in the Rylands Library is, indeed, a precursor to the printed Bibles of today.

3

"If You Know Me"

THE DIVINE CHRIST IN CONTROVERSY

FROM THE second century to the fifth, Christological controversies embroiled Christian communities across North Africa, the eastern Mediterranean, Syria, Asia Minor, and onward toward the western Roman Empire. Was Jesus a human being? Was he divine? Was he a mixture of divine and human? What was his precise relationship to God? If Jesus was divine, are there now two Gods? These questions were deeply interwoven with the language of the Gospel of John and its interpretation. We have already seen the complex ideas about Jesus in the Fourth Gospel. "I and the Father are one," Jesus says, and the opening prologue states unequivocally that "the Word was God." And yet Jesus in this Gospel is also called "rabbi," or teacher, the good shepherd, and the "King of Israel" and "messiah," each of which are titles referring to a human being, not a divine figure. Some second-century Christians appear to have believed that Jesus was completely divine: recall the opponents of the writer of 1 John who seem to have believed that Jesus did not actually exist in flesh and blood. Other Christians used the

Gospels to show that Jesus was a human being, adopted by God at his baptism. Much of what we know about the varieties of Christianity in the earliest centuries suggests that we would do well to speak of Christianity in the plural—*Christianities*. Debates about what constituted heresy and orthodoxy encompassed everything from Christology to what food was proper for Christians to eat, which scriptures were true, what behaviors were proper in churches, whether it was okay to get married or divorced, and whether the world was fundamentally good or evil.

One of the varieties of Christianity in the early period, a form that comes to be labeled "heretical," is what we sometimes call "Gnosticism." Scholars have used the term "Gnosticism"—which is derived from the Greek word for "knowledge," *gnōsis*—as a kind of umbrella term for groups who claimed that the way to salvation was through secret knowledge. But it is worth emphasizing that the term "Gnosticism" itself is a modern construction.[1] We actually do not know the extent to which Christians formed communities around philosophical ideas about *gnōsis,* nor can we say definitively whether gnostic ideas had their origin in various Jewish groups and/or Greek philosophical systems. We do know that some Christians accused other Christians of holding "gnostic" worldviews considered heretical and erroneous. One accusation was that they claimed too high a Christology, a Christology so high that Jesus ceased to be human, their opponents said, and their emphasis on secret *knowledge* raised all sorts of red flags. Who had the authority to decide what was true knowledge, for example? And who are the insiders to secrets? What are the dangers to esoteric knowledge?

Ancient Christian gnostics—I will continue to use the term with caution—appear to have been especially drawn to the Gospel of John and derived some of their ideas from it: recall

John's use of the language of "knowing" throughout the narrative and its vertical Christology (Jesus comes from above, descends to earth). As far as we can tell, the very first Christian commentary written on any biblical book was one written on the Gospel of John by a man named Heracleon, a Christian gnostic. In this chapter, we will explore the early interpretations of the Gospel of John by Christians of different orientations. We will move through such controversies toward the ways in which writers like Augustine interpreted the Gospel of John as "sublime," and how they managed to make such claims in spite of the gnostic affection for the Gospel.

The *Apocryphon of John*

In 1945, an Egyptian farmer made an astonishing discovery in the process of digging for fertilizer near the village of Nag Hammadi along the Nile in upper Egypt: an earthenware jar containing a set of thirteen papyrus books, written in Coptic (the latest form of the Egyptian language). The story of this find has been now told many times. One of the first scholars to study these texts, Elaine Pagels, relays the story from the farmer himself, Muhammad Ali al-Samman:

> Shortly before he and his brothers avenged their father's murder in a blood feud, they had saddled their camels and gone out to the Jabal to dig for *sabakh,* a soft soil they used to fertilize their crops. Digging around a massive boulder, they hit a red earthenware jar, almost a meter high. Muhammad Ali hesitated to break the jar, considering that a *jinn,* or spirit, might live inside. But realizing that it might also contain gold, he raised his mattock, smashed the jar, and discovered inside thirteen papyrus books, bound in leather.[2]

Muhammad Ali's mother burned some of the codices for fuel, but eventually, the remainder of the codices made their way to authorities in Cairo, and some were then sold; scholars in Europe and the US caught wind of the find and were eager to see the codices and decipher them. They have come to be known as the Nag Hammadi Library, and they have enriched our understanding of early Christianity in important ways. The codices themselves are dated to the fourth century, but many of them are translations from Greek texts that were probably written in the second century.

Prior to the find, many of the texts contained in the codices had only been known to scholars from fragmentary papyri or quotations found in the writings of church fathers. But here were the texts themselves, mostly intact—texts like the *Gospel of Truth*, the *Gospel of Thomas*, and the *Gospel of Philip*; treatises such as the *Treatise on the Resurrection*; eschatological texts like the *Apocalypse of Paul*, *Apocalypse of James*, and the *Apocalypse of Adam;* and stories/mythologies of the creation of the world like *The Hypostasis of the Archons*, *On the Origin of the World*, and the *Apocryphon of John*. Four copies of this last text have been discovered: three in the Nag Hammadi codices and one from a closely related archaeological find. To the extent that we can estimate interest and readership of texts by the numbers of copies that remain—a somewhat dubious claim—the multiple copies of the *Apocryphon of John* suggest it may have been quite popular. It surely seems significant that there were three copies of the text among the thirteen codices found at Nag Hammadi.

Scholars continue to debate whether the so-called Nag Hammadi library is an actual library belonging to a community of gnostic-minded individuals or if, perhaps, the proximity of the find at Nag Hammadi to one of the earliest monastic settlements, the Pachomian monastery, suggests another origin for the books. But as a collection, the texts offer us a remarkable opportunity to understand the diversity of early Christianity. The people who wrote and read these texts clearly thought of themselves as Christian: the figure of Jesus emerges in some of them; they speak of rituals like baptism and eucharist; they interpret and reimagine biblical texts. And at the center of many of the Nag Hammadi texts is the Gospel of John and its interpretation. The texts remind us of some of the unusual features of the Gospel itself: the structure of the narrative, Jesus's long speeches, the language of knowing and belief, a Christology that seems to vary widely from low to high, a vertical kind of Christology, and so forth. To illustrate how the Nag Hammadi texts can be viewed in relationship to the Gospel of John, I turn to a close look at one text in particular—namely, the *Apocryphon of John*, whose author, according to the scholar Karen King, "wanted the reader to see a connection" to the Gospel of John.[3]

The *Apocryphon of John* begins, "The teaching of the Savior, and the revelation of the mysteries, and the things hidden in silence, things he taught his disciple John" (*ApJohn* 1:1).[4] We can pause to notice here some key ideas right at the outset—the Savior, Jesus, is identified as a teacher, and he specifically teaches hidden things to his disciple, the same disciple as the one to whom the Fourth Gospel was attributed. Immediately following this esoteric and mysterious beginning the author shifts abruptly to a dialogue between John and a Pharisee named Arimanios, who asks the disciples: "Where is your master whom you followed?" John responds: "He has gone to the place from which he came.' " Arimanios then claims that John has been deceived about "this Nazarene." John immediately heads to the desert to contemplate these things; he finds himself "grieved" trying to understand why "the Savior" was sent into the world. "Why was he sent into the world by his Father?

Who is his Father who sent him? To what kind of eternal realm shall we go?" John asks. The relationship to the Fourth Gospel—which speaks of "the world" and a Jesus sent from the father—is apparent here. To some extent, the *Apocryphon of John* can be read as a riff on the Fourth Gospel, especially its opening. One way of reading this text is, according to King, that the *Apocryphon of John* "is filling the gaps in Christ's revelation in the *Gospel of John,* offering a fuller narrative of the Divine Realm, the creation of the world and humanity, the condition of humanity in the world, and salvation."[5]

In this text, John receives a revelation from a figure "within the light"—suggesting another connection to the Gospel of John, which repeatedly speaks of light and darkness.

> John, John, why are you doubting? Why are you afraid? Aren't you familiar with this figure? Then do not be fainthearted. I am with you always. I am the Father, I am the Mother, I am the Child. I am the incorruptible and the undefiled one. Now I have come to teach you what is, what was, and what is going to come, that you may understand what is invisible and what is visible. (*ApJohn* 2:9–18)

The figure, who is subsequently identified as the Savior, then gives a lengthy revelation about "the One": the "God and Parent, Father of the All, the invisible one that is over the All, that is incorruptible, that is pure light at which no eye can gaze." The Savior speaks of the origin of the world, offers a retelling of the story of Adam and Eve, and describes Adam who "became a mortal person, the first to descend and the first to become estranged" (*ApJohn* 21:13).

This language of above (and below) is crucial for understanding the cosmology and theology of both the *Apocryphon of John* and the Fourth Gospel. We often think of the apocalyptic worldview as a linear view of time and the prophetic unfolding of events: a past, a present crisis, a future catastrophe and a reckoning, a final judgment day. But in the gnostic framework, the unfolding of time seems embedded within a vertical cosmology: the one great unknowable divine is in the heavens above, separated from humans down here on earth. Over time and through a series of events, fragments of that divine domain come to "fall" to the earth and embed themselves within some humans, who then need to search for the origin of these divine sparks so that they can reunite them with their heavenly home. With its focus on the creation of the world and mortal beings, this text offers detailed expansion on the first words of the Gospel of John (and Genesis): "In the beginning" (Genesis 1:1; John 1:1). What happened in the beginning of time? According to the *Apocryphon of John*, "everything has come into being" (another allusion to John) by means of the "Invisible Spirit." It's as though the author has braided together a cosmology and soteriology built of Genesis, John, and a gnostic worldview. Above all, and for our purposes, the *Apocryphon of John* can be read as one of the many legacies of the Gospel of John, and an early reworking of some of the key themes of the Fourth Gospel.

Heracleon's Commentary on John

We can approach the early appropriation and interpretation of the Gospel of John through another kind of text—namely, the commentary tradition. The earliest Christian commentary written on the Fourth Gospel was one written by man named Heracleon around the year 170 CE. What is most striking about this is that Heracleon was regarded as a heretic by proto-orthodox Christians because his ideas were gnostic in their orientation.

Our knowledge of Heracleon is quite limited since his commentary has not survived. We can, however, reconstruct some of his interpretation of the Gospel of John through the writings of one of his opponents, a third-century Christian philosopher from Alexandria, Egypt named Origen, who was also eventually declared a heretic.[6] Origen was a Christian theologian and exegete; he also was a teacher, instructing new converts to Christianity. If the landscape of heresy and orthodoxy in early Christianity seems confusing and complicated, that's because it was. Christians disagreed on everything from who Jesus was to how to conduct baptisms, which texts were to be considered sacred scripture, the relationship between Jewish and Christian practices, and many other issues. The earliest centuries were a chaotic time as diverse views led to all sorts of debates and schisms.

To return to Heracleon: somewhat before Origen, Irenaeus—the bishop from Lyon, France, writing in the late second century—had already described some of Heracleon's ideas in relationship to a group called the Valentinians, a group of Christians who followed a gnostic teacher named Valentinus. One of the key claims made by Heracleon and other Valentinians concerns the very idea embedded in the Gospel of John—in particular, the notion that the "Word became flesh," that Jesus was truly flesh and blood. But their ideas, according to Pagels, were not an outright dispute of the humanness of Jesus. She writes,

> Gnostic theologians do not necessarily *deny* that the events proclaimed of Jesus have occurred in history. What they deny is that the actuality of these events matter *theologically*. Heracleon, claims, for example, that those who insist that Jesus, a man who lived "in the flesh," is "Christ" fail to distinguish between literal and symbolic truth. Those who write

> accounts of the revelation as alleged biographies of "Jesus of Nazareth"—or even of Jesus as the Messiah—focus on mere historical "externals" and miss the inner truth they signify.[7]

This notion of Gnostics searching for the inner truth, the hidden meaning of things, resonates with the very opening of the *Apocryphon of John*. These were dangerous ideas, it seems. After all, who has the authority to decide what these hidden meanings are and how the secret symbolism should be interpreted?

In Origen's *Commentary on the Gospel of John*, he refers to Heracleon's commentary some fifty times, and he quotes from it extensively. We cannot, of course, treat Origen's quotations from Heracleon's commentary with complete confidence, for Origen (like Irenaeus and others) viewed Heracleon as a heretic. But this is our best evidence for understanding Heracleon's views regarding the Fourth Gospel. Origen's refutation of Heracleon's ideas appears in his own commentary on the Gospel of John, produced in the third century. A couple of passages from Origen's commentary on the Gospel of John where he quotes from Heracleon help to illustrate what this earliest Christian commentator on John appears to have said.

Take, for example, the passage in John 1:3, "All things were made through him, and without him nothing was made." Origen writes,

> It was, I consider, a violent and unwarranted procedure which was adopted by Heracleon, the friend, as it is said, of Valentinus in discussing this sentence: "All things were made through Him." He excepted the whole world and all that it contains, excluding, as far as his hypothesis goes, from the "all things" what is best in the world and its contents. For he says that the aeon [the age], and the things in it, were not made by the Logos [the Word]; he considers them to have

> come into existence before the Logos. He deals with the statement, "without Him was nothing made," with some degree of audacity. (*Commentary on John* 2.8)[8]

What's going on here? This is a debate about the role of the Logos, the Word. When the Gospel of John begins with "in the beginning was the Word" and then says, "all things were made through him" (or "all things came into being through him") it raises the fundamental question of the creation of the world. Who was responsible for the creation of the world? And what were, exactly, all the things that were created at the beginning? Was the Word created? Or did the Word assist in the creation of the world? Origen is providing an important insight into one gnostic idea, for gnostics seemed to have thought that the material world was largely evil, that the good divine world from above had become trapped in a physical world below that was filled with evil and suffering. So how could Christ, the Word, the Logos be responsible for creating such a problematic world? Some gnostics thought that there was a lesser god, a demiurge, who must have been responsible for the creation of the material world. And Origen finds this an audacious claim.

Let's look at one more example from Heracleon's commentary, this one taken from his interpretation of John 2:13–16, the story of Jesus going up to Jerusalem, entering the Temple, and throwing out the money changers and those selling livestock. Heracleon, according to Origen, interprets this passage like this: "The ascent to Jerusalem signifies the ascent of the Lord from material things to the spiritual place, which is a likeness of Jerusalem." So far, so good. Heracleon is reading the passage in light of a gnostic cosmology: the universe divided into the spiritual realm above and the earthly realm below. But Origen continues to recount how Heracleon uses the words "in the temple, he found" to describe another metaphysical distinction, now based on the physical structure of the Temple. Heracleon interprets the "temple" as the "Holy of Holies," Origen says, and this leads him to make a distinction again between those who are spiritual who can enter this most sacred realm and those who are not. Furthermore, Heracleon interpets the whip that Jesus wields in the Fourth Gospel as "an image of the power and energy of the Holy Spirit, driving out by His breath those who are bad" (*Commentary on John* 10:19). What is Origen's opposition to Heracleon's interpretation really about? Nothing less than the very meaning of scripture. If one believes scripture to be sacred and authoritative, then it matters that its interpretation is correct. If every word of scripture is laden with meaning, who determines what the meaning is? Heracleon has adopted a symbolic reading of passages like Jesus's cleansing of the Temple that Origen finds "exceedingly distorted" and "obviously absurd."

Origen's commentary on the Gospel of John is important for our understanding of Heracleon's views, but it also provides a rich illustration of the level of detail of the text that could be interpreted. As Joseph Trigg has suggested, Origen "not only paid critical attention to the meaning of the words in the manner of Alexandrian scholarship, but compared each significant word or concept in the text at hand with that word or concept as it appears elsewhere in scripture."[9] The wording was important, yes, but also the punctuation and grammatical structures. It appears that it took five volumes for Origen to comment on just the first seventeen verses of the Gospel of John!

Throughout his commentary, Origen observes that different manuscripts of the Gospel of John sometimes have different readings and that there were scribal errors in these manuscripts. Take, for example, the last verse of John's prologue: "No one has ever seen God at any time, but *the unique Son/the unique God* who is in the bosom of the Father, that one has made him known" (Jn 1:18). This is a grammatically awkward verse and it is rendered into English in multiple different ways, including the common mistranslation of the Greek word for "unique" as "only-begotten." The textual problem lies in a difference of one word: some manuscripts read that it was "the unique Son," while others read that it was "the unique God" who is in the "bosom of the Father." Origen's interpretation of this verse suggests that he was using manuscripts that read "unique God."[10] Every detail, no matter how small, was important. A single word could make a world of difference. And this is a good example of how what seems like a simple textual variant, as we call differences between manuscripts, has implications for Christology and theology: at stake in the matters is no less than whether Jesus is God.

For a long time scholars argued for a distinction between two centers of Christian interpretation: Alexandria and Antioch. And they suggested that these two locations produced two main types of interpretation—the Alexandrian mode was to use allegory for interpretation; the Antiochene mode, on the other hand, was more historical and typological. The distinction does not hold very well, for interpretation very frequently does not fit into categories nor does it map neatly on to locations, but it is important to recognize the various hermeneutical strategies that Christians employed. Much of Origen's own interpretation can be read as allegorical. Allegory, as Averil Cameron has suggested, was in part a "rhetorical device. Figural imagery was embedded in the language of the Bible, and its exploitation by commentators made possible an acceptable presentation of Christian ideas to outsiders as well as of the Old Testament to Christians."[11] For an erudite scholar like

Origen—and before him Jewish philosophers and biblical interpreters like Philo of Alexandria—reading the Bible only literally was to lose its true meaning. Origen claims that there are three different levels or meaning in scripture: the first level is the literal reading, the second level is the moral, and the third is the spiritual meaning. He reads these levels of meaning as the body, soul, and spirit of scripture; these levels can in turn be associated with different kinds of readers. Take, for example, his commentary on the story of Jesus and the Samaritan woman from John 4. Trigg notes how for Origen,

> The story reveals three possible approaches to Scripture: that of the heretics, which is utterly false; that of simple Christians, which is very limited; that of spiritual Christians, which offers the possibility of mystical communion with God. The Samaritan woman, Origen believed, was a heretic whom Jesus redeemed from her error. . . . While the literal sense is patent to all believing Christians, the mystical sense, the true meaning John intended, is open only to those who have been given the grace to receive it.[12]

Origen did not mince words when it came to denouncing the interpretations of his opponents, especially gnostics like Heracleon or Valentinus; he drew sharp distinctions between his own allegorical readings and what he regarded as the fantastic speculations of the gnostics.

By contrast, John Chrysostom, who was born in Antioch and served as archbishop of Constantinople in the late fourth century, took a much more literal approach to the text of the Gospel of John in his sermons; he also speaks directly to his congregation as he explains the meaning of a passage. Take, for example, Chrysostom's homily on John 1:9: "The true light, which enlightens everyone, was coming into the world." About this passage, John Chrysostom asks: "If He 'enlightens everyone' how is it that so many continue unenlightened?" He continues: "some willfully close the eyes of their mind," not because of the light itself, but because of their own "wickedness." He goes on to say that the light was given to everyone as a gift and it is only human "wickedness" that leads some to not accept the light as a grace, a gift (*Homily* 7.1). On this same passage, Origen describes the "light" of John 1:9 in an altogether different way: "the sensible light of the world is the sun," he writes, "and after it comes very worthily the moon, and the same title may be applied to the stars . . . but the Savior shines on creatures which have intellect and sovereign reason, that their minds may behold their proper objects of vision, and so he is the light of the intellectual world, that is to say, of the reasonable souls which are in the sensible world" (*Commentary on John* 1.9). Chrysostom reads the passage in a way that has a moral teaching for his congregation (i.e., about wickedness); Origen's reading is much more philosophical as he turns to reason and intellect and how the light speaks to these qualities in the world.

The impulse toward commentaries (and sermons) in the early period was in part born of a desire to refute opponents' views. Origen, as we have seen, is working to refute Heracleon. Chrysostom's sermons speak directly against those he calls "heretics." As William Lamb has suggested,

> the sheer volume of the number of commentaries on John and the startling differences between them demonstrate that the Gospel of John remained contested territory. Controversies over a whole range of exegetical questions in the course of the first five centuries played their part in stimulating the development of Christian doctrine and the making of orthodoxy.[13]

Interpretation did not take place in a vacuum; it was inextricably linked to the diversity of Christian ideas about faith, belief, Jesus, and God. And diverse views did not disappear once commentaries were written. Nor did they disappear when Christians began writing creeds, which were also produced as a mechanism to resolve controversies once and for all. The most well-known early creed is one that was written in Nicaea, Asia Minor, in the year 325. The Nicene Creed was produced by an ecumenical church council called, at least in part, to deal with Arianism, a form of Christianity that claimed that God the Father has existed forever, but Christ the Son was "begotten" or "made" before time by God. We can see how the language of the Gospel of John, especially in the various readings at John 1:18, played a role in such controversies. Was Jesus co-eternal with the Father or was there a time that Jesus came into being? Although the impact of the Nicene Creed was enormous—it serves, after all, as the basis for later creedal formulations—it did not end the Arian controversy, nor did it end Christological debates. In the fifth century the North African bishop Augustine was delivering his sermons on the Gospel of John, and he also speaks directly against the Arians.

Augustine and the Fourth Gospel

The biography of Augustine of Hippo, the bishop of Hippo in North Africa roughly from 395–430 CE, has been written many times, so this summary can be brief. He also left his own autobiography, *The Confessions*, which tells of his conversion to an ascetic form of Christianity. He was born in 354 CE at Thagaste, a town in what is now Algeria, to a Christian mother, and his language was Latin, which had now supplanted Greek as the language of literature, philosophy, and religion in the western

Mediterranean, and he was educated in rhetoric. North Africa, as elsewhere in the Mediterranean, had seen its share of Christological controversies by the time of Augustine, and he writes and delivers sermons with frequent reference to various movements, including the Arians. The Manichaeans—followers of the third-century teacher Mani—espoused a strictly dualistic and extreme form of asceticism, the practices and beliefs associated with denying the body pleasure.

Monasticism was flourishing in the Christianity of this period: the stories of hermits going out into the desert to dedicate themselves to an ascetic life of celibacy and solitude were being written; communal monasteries where groups of monks or nuns could live together were being built. In his *Confessions*, Augustine speaks about his turn toward the ascetic life—not the severe form taught by Mani, but to a life of committed celibacy. His interpretation of scripture was fundamentally shaped by this conversion as he inflected his sermons, treatises, letters, and commentaries with ascetic ideals.[14] What is striking, too, about his approach, especially in his sermons on the Gospel of John, is his use of allegorical interpretations—he searches for the hidden meanings within the text. Augustine, according to John Rettig, became devoted to going beyond a literal understanding of scripture:

> In John's Gospel, even more than the rest of Scripture, the literal and historical realities of Christ's life represent spiritual reality. Each specific historical act is significant of an interior, hidden, more real action; each specific historical act reveals a universalization pertinent to the inner spiritual life of the human soul.[15]

This does not mean that Augustine was a strict allegorist; rather, he has an expansive view of interpretation. For Augustine, "the signs of Scripture function properly when they rightly direct our attention to the Trinity."[16]

Augustine was prolific in his interpretation of scripture, writing commentaries, sermons, letters, treatises, major theological works, and so on. He was steeped in scripture and immersed in the world of citation and explication: "For Augustine," William Harmless writes, "the Bible's words were food, were life itself."[17] And he turned time and time again to the Gospel of John. Harmless continues: "Augustine loved John's Gospel for its sublimity. 'The evangelist John,' he once told his congregation, 'soars to greater heights like an eagle; he transcends the murky darkness of earth; he looks upon the light of truth with a steadier gaze.'"[18]

The Gospel of John offered Augustine an opportunity to understand the deep meaning of Jesus's words and deeds. Take, for example, the following passage from a sermon where he talks about the differences between the Synoptic Gospels and the Gospel of John:

> For the other three evangelists [Matthew, Mark, Luke], walked with the Lord on earth as with a man; concerning His divinity they have said but little; but this evangelist [John], as if he disdained to walk on earth, just as in the very opening of his discourse he thundered on us, soared not only above the earth and above the whole compass of air and sky, but even above the whole army of angels and the whole order of invisible powers, and reached to Him by whom all things were made; saying, "In the beginning was the Word, and the Word was with God, and the Word was God. This was in the beginning with God. All things were made by Him, and without Him nothing was made" [Jn 1:1–3]. To this so great sublimity of his beginning all the rest of his preaching

> well agrees; and he has spoken concerning the divinity of the Lord as none other has spoken. What he had drank in, the same he gave forth. For it is not without reason that it is recorded of him in this very Gospel, that at supper he reclined on the Lord's bosom. From that breast then he drank in secret; but what he drank in secret he gave forth openly, that there may come to all nations not only the incarnation of the Son of God, and His passion and resurrection, but also what He was before His incarnation, the only Son of the Father, the Word of the Father, co-eternal with Him that begot, equal with Him by whom He was sent; but yet in that very sending made less, that the Father might be greater. (*Tractates on the Gospel of John* 36.1)[19]

I have quoted this long passage to provide a feel for how Augustine works with the Fourth Gospel, and because it reveals something important about the fifth century: debates about the origin of Jesus and about his relationship to God—the Son and the Father—continue to swirl even in this period. In many ways, this is one of the most important legacies of the Gospel of John: how Christians read this text deeply shaped their ideas about the Trinity (Father, Son, Holy Spirit), about the role of Christ at the beginning of time ("In the beginning"), and about Christ's nature as both divine and human. Augustine, as with earlier interpreters, is responding to those he regards as heretics. He recognizes problems like the fact that the Synoptics are so different from the Fourth Gospel, but he singles John out for its sublimity and openness and above all for the way it speaks of Jesus's divinity. The council at Nicaea had tried to resolve the issue of Jesus's identity by establishing a creed that declared he was "truly God and truly man," but this was not the end of debate, as Augustine shows.

Countless examples of the way that Augustine allegorizes the Gospel of John could be given. Every word, every phrase has a mystery, a deeper meaning. To show some of how he accomplishes this, we can turn to a passage from the Gospel of John that was problematic in the first century and was the crux of some of the Reformation debates. The passage is from John 6:

> Jesus said to them, "Very truly, I tell you, unless you eat the flesh of the Son of Man and drink his blood, you have no life in you. Those who eat my flesh and drink my blood have eternal life, and I will raise them up on the last day; for my flesh is true food and my blood is true drink. Those who eat my flesh and drink my blood abide in me, and I in them." (6:53–56)

In this passage, the disciples and those around him find it difficult to understand this teaching, given that it sounds like cannibalism. Eating his flesh and drinking his blood? Here is how Augustine handles the passage: Jesus wants, Augustine says, "this food and drink to be understood as the society of his body and his members, that which is the holy Church in its saints who were predestined, and called, and justified, and glorified, and in its believers" (*Tractates* 26.15). Augustine moves next to the Eucharist: "The sacrament of this reality, that is, of the unity of the body and blood of Christ, is provided at the Lord's table, in some places daily, in other places with certain intervals of days" (26.15). So food and drink can represent the Christian church itself, yes, but the passage also offers an opportunity for Augustine to talk about various church practices vis-à-vis the Eucharist. These ideas will resurface in our inquiry into how the Fourth Gospel shaped the Protestant Reformation, for Martin Luther's interpretation of scripture was particularly indebted to the Gospel of John and especially to

Augustine's reading of the Gospel of John. The interpretation of this passage and the meaning of the Eucharist will serve to divide Christians in the sixteenth century. Christian history layers itself as one exegete after another turns to reread and reinterpret the Gospel of John.

Conclusion

The goal of this chapter has been to see how the Gospel of John both contributed to and was mobilized in response to Christian controversies and debates. The received tradition about early Christian diversity is that there was one true faith, one correct belief, that extended all the way back to Jesus, who transmitted it to his disciples, who took it to various parts of the world. Along the way, in this view, some Christians departed from this correct belief: heresies arose as a kind of offshoot from true faith. Ever since the time of Eusebius, the first church historian who was based in Caesarea in the early fourth century, Christians had claimed that there was one true and orthodox Christian faith stretching back to Jesus himself (and even earlier!) and that along the way, there were those who made claims (and even gathered followers) that strayed from the one true teaching—these were heretics and they were to be shunned, expelled, condemned. One of the key points of contention had to do with these heretical views about who Jesus was, or, more precisely, about Christology. Was Jesus human? Was he divine? Was he a combination of both?

But over the course of the twentieth century, scholars of the New Testament and early Christianity have shifted away from this received Christian tradition about heresy and orthodoxy. The Nag Hammadi Library has complicated this view, for it provides us with very early Christian ideas about the divine world, about Jesus, and about the creation that came only later to be considered heretical. When we look at the first and second centuries—the origins of Christianity—we find that diverse views existed from the very beginning. The diversity of views come to be regarded as a problem, as something to be opposed. The Gospel of John was mobilized in the service of articulating a wide range of views. If we place the *Apocryphon of John* next to the commentaries of Origen and look closely at the sermons of Chrysostom and Augustine, what we find is a continual struggle. Indeed, although Christianity is often regarded as a "doctrinal religion"—and it does come to establish creeds and doctrines—the diversity from the earliest period speaks to a kind of elasticity. The Gospel of John is, perhaps remarkably, at the forefront of the pull and push of interpreting scripture and articulating "true faith."

4

"Fear of the Jews"

JOHN AND THE LEGACIES OF ANTISEMITISM

ONE OF the most contentious and controversial aspects of the Gospel of John is, as I've already intimated, its insistent use of the phrase "the Jews" (in Greek: *hoi ioudaioi*). This phrase is one of the most distinctive features of the Fourth Gospel, its message, and its subsequent interpretation. To put the issue into simple perspective: the phrase *hoi ioudaioi* is used nearly seventy times in the Gospel of John; by contrast, the Synoptic Gospels each use the phrase no more than six times. Moreover, the majority of the instances of the phrase in John are negative and hostile—the characters identified as "the Jews," as we have seen, are increasingly opposed to Jesus, they seek to kill him, and they call for his crucifixion. The sheer ubiquity of the phrase in the Fourth Gospel as well as its bias requires explanation. We can begin with an understanding of how the phrase was used more generally in antiquity.

The Meaning of *hoi ioudaioi*

It might seem as though the term "Jews" (*ioudaioi*) was commonly used to identify the religious group whose scriptures promoted monotheism, whose temple was located in Jerusalem, and whose people gathered in synagogues to read from the Torah, the scriptures. But the picture is far more complicated. Stretching back into the earliest stages of the Bible, we actually find that the terms used to identify Yahweh worshippers were "sons of Israel," "Israelites," "Israel," or, even earlier, "the Hebrews." These terms are used thousands of times in the biblical corpus. The Greek word *ioudaios* in its various forms, on the other hand, comes into use in the Hellenistic period as a way of translating the Aramaic and Hebrew word *Yehuda*, Judah, or Judea—a person, one of the sons of Jacob and the leader of the tribe of Judah; and a place, Jerusalem and its surrounding region. It also comes to be used to refer to a people, Jews, collectively. During the Hellenistic period, and in the aftermath of exile and the conquests of Alexander, *ioudaioi* is used more frequently and likewise it is used with greater frequency in the Greek translations of the later books of the Hebrew Bible.

In the New Testament, the phrase *hoi ioudaioi* appears in Matthew, Mark, and Luke in the phrase "king of the Jews," which was used to identify Jesus at his birth, during his trial, and on the plaque placed on his cross: "Over his head they put the charge against him, which read, 'This is Jesus, the King of the Jews'" (Mt 27:37; Mk 15:26; Lk 23:38). It also occurs in the Gospel of Mark as a kind of parenthetical remark to explain why some Pharisees and scribes were concerned that Jesus's disciples were not washing their hands before eating: "For the Pharisees, and all the Jews, do not eat unless they thoroughly wash their hands" (Mk 7:3). There is no negative bias against "the Jews" specifically in these Gospels, which tend instead to use terms like "Pharisees," "Sadducees," "scribes," and/or "priests" to identify specific Jewish groups who oppose Jesus; so, too, the Synoptics speak of "the crowds" or "the people" around Jesus who sometimes oppose him. "The Jews" is a decidedly neutral phrase in the Synoptics. The contrast with the Fourth Gospel could not be more striking.

In the Gospel of John, "the Jews" or the singular "Jew" occurs frequently and with a growing negative bias. There are instances where we might regard the term as neutral: for example, when it's used to refer to Jewish festivals, as in "The Passover of the Jews was near" (Jn 2:13) or "After this there was a festival of the Jews, and Jesus went up to Jerusalem" (Jn 5:1). It is also used without overtly negative overtones to refer to individuals, such as Nicodemus (Jn 3:1). Then there are the roles of "the Jews" in questioning Jesus and his disciples on matters of Jewish practice: in the passage we examined in the last chapter, for example, "the Jews" question Jesus's claim that he is the bread of life (Jn 6:41). There are instances of "the Jews" believing Jesus's message, such as "the Jews" who witness Jesus raising Lazarus from the dead (Jn 11:45). And importantly, Jesus himself is identified as a "Jew" in the story of his encounter with the Samaritan woman who asks: "How is it that you, a Jew, ask a drink of me, a woman of Samaria?" she asks Jesus, "for Jews have no dealings with Samaritans" (Jn 4:9).

But the most vivid and frequent use of "the Jews" in the Fourth Gospel betrays a troubling bias: "The Jews" accuse Jesus of having a demon (Jn 8:52); "The Jews took up stones against to stone him" (Jn 10:31); "the Jews" demand Jesus's death (Jn 19:7); and throughout the Gospel the "fear of the Jews" occurs several times (e.g., Jn 9:22). When Jesus heals a sick man in

Jerusalem, "the Jews started persecuting Jesus, because he was doing such things on the sabbath" (Jn 5:16). And the story continues: "For this reason the Jews were seeking all the more to kill him, because he was not only breaking the sabbath, but was also calling God his own Father, thereby making himself equal to God" (Jn 5:19). If we compare this to a very similar passage in the Gospel of Matthew we see the distinctiveness, for in Matthew we find, "But the Pharisees went out and conspired against him, how to destroy him" (Mt 12:14). Here, Matthew focuses the attention on the Pharisees, while John expands to "the Jews."

Even more striking is the story of Jesus's trial before Pilate in the Gospel of John. To be sure, the Synoptics include the story of the trial and they speak of the "crowds," "the chief priests," or "all the people" who are calling for Jesus's crucifixion. Pilate in the Synoptics "wonders" about the accusations (e.g., Mk 15:5) or he says simply "I find no crime in this man," which is followed in Luke with chief priests and the crowds urging Pilate to crucify him and then the story of Pilate sending Jesus to Herod (Lk 23:1–12). Jesus stays mostly quiet during the trial in the Synoptics, responding "you say so" to Pilate's queries. By contrast, in John the narrative of the trial unfolds dramatically with a Jesus who is much more vocal. And the key characters who are calling for Jesus's crucifixion are "the Jews": after Pilate brings Jesus out to the people wearing a crown of thorns and purple robe, "the chief priests and the police" shout, "Crucify him, crucify him" (Jn 19:6). But look at what follows:

> Pilate said to them, "Take him yourselves and crucify him; I find no case against him." *The Jews* answered him, "We have a law, and by that law he ought to die, because he has claimed to be the Son of God." Now when Pilate heard this, he was more afraid than ever. He entered his headquarters again and

> asked Jesus, "Where are you from?" But Jesus gave him no answer. Pilate therefore said to him, "Do you refuse to speak to me? Do you not know that I have power to release you, and power to crucify you?" Jesus answered him, "You would have no power over me unless it had been given you from above; therefore the one who handed me over to you is guilty of a greater sin." From then on Pilate tried to release him, but *the Jews* cried out, "If you release this man, you are no friend of the emperor. Everyone who claims to be a king sets himself against the emperor." (Jn 19:6–12)

Notice here how the narrator has depicted a Pilate who is reluctant and only acquiesces to the insistence of "the Jews," who are mentioned twice. The legacy of this passage is significant: by the middle of the second century, we find Christian sermons that are delivered with the explicit message that Jews killed Jesus and that is why their Temple was destroyed. This will be the dominant Christian interpretation down through the reformation and into the present day. For example, Martin Luther, in his sixteenth-century sermons on the Gospel of John, writes: "Christ . . . is God himself. When I touch Him, see Him, and physically crucify Him, *as the Jews did,* I am touching God" (*Sermons on the Gospel of John* 33, 158–159, emphasis added).

John's use of the phrase "the Jews" is not arbitrary or incidental to the story; the specific use of this phrase is quite deliberate. And it cannot be easily dismissed as some kind of geographical marker. Although *hoi ioudaioi* could be translated as "the Judeans," the problem with this translation is that the phrase is used in John for those in Galilee, not just those in Judea. I agree with New Testament scholar Adele Reinhartz, who claims:

> The negative characterization of the Jews, especially their hostility and violence towards Jesus and his followers,

> implies a rhetorical intention on the part of the Gospel: to encourage its audience to distance themselves from the label *ioudaios* and from those non-believers to whom that label is applied.[1]

The cumulative effect of this usage of "the Jews" in this Gospel raises important questions. To what extent is the author deliberately trying to distinguish Jesus from Jews, or perhaps from his own Jewishness? Or, as Reinhartz asks: "Why would a Gospel that situates its story so firmly in a Jewish social, cultural, political, geographical, and conceptual landscape at the same time distance its protagonist and thereby its audience from an identification as or with the Jews?"[2] What purpose does distancing Jesus from his own Jewishness serve? One explanation that has been given, as we have already seen, is that the rhetoric of the Fourth Gospel may at least in part derive from the history of the community behind the Gospel, a community that may have begun within synagogues, developed conflict with those in synagogues about their views of Jesus, and was subsequently banned from the synagogues. The expelled Jesus followers then began to develop a hostility toward the Jews who remained behind, who did not believe in Jesus, and as more Gentiles (non-Jews) began joining with this expelled group, the hostility increased. This explanation almost certainly oversimplifies the historical developments in the first century, but it continues to persuade many scholars.

John 8:44 and its Interpretation

The most violent passage in the Gospel of John, aside from the story of Jesus's trial and crucifixion, is perhaps the one contained in John 8. It's worth quoting in full as we delve into the legacy of the Fourth Gospel's anti-Judaism. The context of the exchange between Jesus and "the Jews" is Jesus's teaching about his identity: "I am the light of the world. Whoever follows me will never walk in darkness but will have the light of life" (Jn 8:12). The Pharisees then question Jesus about this saying. In response he says, "I am going away and you will search for me, but you will die in your sin" (Jn 8:21). The whole passage is about who the true descendants of Abraham are and how Jesus is indeed the one sent by God, the Father. The tension escalates between Jesus and "the Jews" as he says these things, and then it culminates in the following:

> Then Jesus said to the Jews who had believed in him, "If you continue in my word, you are truly my disciples, and you will know the truth, and the truth will make you free." They answered him, "We are descendants of Abraham, and have never been slaves to anyone. What do you mean by saying, 'You will be made free'?" Jesus answered them, "Very truly, I tell you, everyone who commits sin is a slave to sin. The slave does not have a permanent place in the household; the son has a place there forever. So if the Son makes you free, you will be free indeed. I know that you are descendants of Abraham; yet you look for an opportunity to kill me, because there is no place in you for my word. I declare to you what I have seen in the Father's presence; as for you, you should do what you have heard from the Father." They answered him, "Abraham is our father." Jesus said them, "If you were Abraham's children, you would be doing what Abraham did, but now you are trying to kill me, a man who has told you the truth that I heard from God. This is not what Abraham did. You are indeed doing what your father did." They said to him, "We were not illegitimate children; we have one father, God

> himself." Jesus said to them, "If God were your Father, you would love me, for I came from God and now I am here. I did not come on my own, but he sent me. Why do you not understand what I say? It is because you cannot accept my word. *You are from your father the devil, and you choose to do your father's desires. He was a murderer from the beginning and does not stand in the truth, because there is no truth in him. When he lies, he speaks according to his own nature, for he is a liar and the father of lies.*" (Jn 8:31–44, emphasis added)

On one level this passage can be read as a debate about ancestry, about "the Jews" and their relationship to Abraham and God. But look closely at the conclusion of the passage: here Jesus says that they are the children of the devil who was a murderer and a liar. This is not a simple quarrel over who is legitimately the descendant of Abraham; it turns to something far more sinister. To explain the full history of Christian ideas about the devil goes beyond our scope here, but I do want to draw out the implications and impact of the passage.[3]

The passage certainly resonated with gnostic ideas about the devil and an evil creator god: April DeConick has suggested that "for the Gnostic Christian, it was gospel proof—the very words of Jesus—that the God of the Jews was a lesser demonic god different from the Father-God whom Jesus preached."[4] Although one of the earliest interpretations of the passage comes in the Johannine Epistles (1 Jn 3:7–10), where "the Jews" have been removed and the distinction is made, instead, between those who have left the community who are called children of the devil, while those who remain are the children of God, the history of the passage's interpretation reveals a violent anti-Jewish and, subsequently, a decidedly antisemitic ideology. John Chrysostom alludes to the passage when he condemns

Christians in Antioch who participate in synagogue life: he says they are acting like the children of demons, children of the devil.[5] Augustine uses the verse in part to counter the Manichaeans, but notice his acceptance of the idea that Jews were children of the devil in the following:

> How, then, were the Jews the children of the devil? By imitation, not by birth. Listen to the usual language of the Holy Scriptures. The prophet says to those very Jews, "Your father was an Amorite, and your mother a Hittite." The Amorites were not a nation that gave origin to the Jews. The Hittites also were themselves of a nation altogether different from the race of the Jews. But because the Amorites and Hittites were impious, and the Jews imitated their impieties, they found parents for themselves, not of whom they were born, but in whose damnation they should share, because they were following their customs. (*Tractates on the Gospel of John* 42.10)

Look at what Augustine is doing here: he is drawing from the prophet Ezekiel, who was condemning "those very Jews" for being the children of Amorites and Hittites, who were not Israelites. The phrase "the Jews" is not found in Ezekiel, but rather the term "Jerusalem." This is a good example of how Christian hermeneutics work: a passage from the Old Testament is woven with a passage from the New Testament to create a tapestry that fits the occasion of Augustine's sermon—the refutation of the Manichaeans and, simultaneously, a condemnation of his congregants for their errors.

We will turn to the Protestant Reformation in the next chapter, but it is worth noting here that Martin Luther will use John 8:44 to condemn Jews, and when he does so, he draws on a wide array of tropes in combination with Johannine ideas: "they are venomous," he says, "bitter, vindictive, tricky serpents, assassins, and children of the devil who sting and work harm stealthily wherever they cannot do it openly."[6] The violent legacy of John 8:44, and the Fourth Gospel's language about "the Jews" more generally, can be brought vividly into the modern period. In the twentieth century, the Nazi children's book *The Poisonous Mushroom*, for example, includes the following:

> Children, look there! The Man who hangs of the Cross was one of the greatest enemies of the Jews of all time. He knew the Jews in all their corruption and meanness. Once He drove the Jews out with a whip, because they were carrying on their money-dealings in the Church. He called the Jews: killers of men from the beginning. By that He meant that the Jews in all times have been murderers. He said further to the Jews: Your father is the Devil! Do you know, children, what that means? It means that the Jews descend from the Devil.[7]

This passage has a mix of two Johannine elements: the story of Jesus with the whip of cords in the Temple, taken from John chapter 2, as well as the passage from John 8:44. Other children's picture books begin with a genealogy that reads: "The Father of the Jews is the Devil"; some include the claim that "the Jew" is "the devil in human form."[8] Such claims, especially in children's literature, may be shocking to those unfamiliar with them. They serve as disturbing reminders of the manifold ways interpreters mobilize scripture to serve their own interests.

During the aftermath of the Holocaust, the International Council of Christians and Jews in 1947 published a document called *The Ten Points of Seelisberg,* which among other things called for Christians to "avoid using the word *Jews* in the exclusive sense of the enemies of Jesus, and the words *The Enemies of Jesus* to designate the whole Jewish people."[9] Yet the use of John 8:44 for antisemitic purposes continues: in the white supremacist march in 2017 in Charlottesville, Virginia, for example, Jews were called "Satan's children." Similarly, Kathleen Elkins has pointed out that "the perpetrator of the Tree of Life shooting in Pittsburgh, Pennsylvania in 2018 used John 8:44 as part of his social media profile."[10] The legacy of John 8:44 continues to reverberate in dangerous and violent antisemitic ways today, so it is particularly surprising that Pope Francis chose to use this verse in his "Letter to the Catholics of the Middle East" on the one-year anniversary of the Hamas attack on Israel. Although his intent was to condemn war as "murderous from the beginning," his explicit reference to John 8:44 served to undermine his message in unsettling ways.[11]

To some extent the legacies of John 8:44 I have provided are all from the viewpoint of dominant voices: the narrator of John, Jesus himself, writers of Nazi children stories, and so forth. But in recent years, scholars and theologians who study how the Bible is used in colonial contexts have encouraged us to see biblical passages such as these from the oppressed viewpoint. Musa Dube and Jeffrey Staley, for example, have argued that "victims of colonialism will read from a variety of time settings and often will identify with 'unorthodox' characters of the biblical text."[12] Mary Huie-Jolly has written about one particular example: she writes that "at the beginning of the twentieth century, certain Maori who had earlier been regarded as converts of the missionaries, now in response to colonial practices which undermined their tribal lands and way of life, called themselves 'Jews' and began to leave the way of the Son."[13] Such an example reveals how the Gospel of John can be read subversively. To identify with "the Jews" of John resists the narrative's force. It also raises the question of identification among contemporary readers who may see themselves as the very characters John wishes to condemn.

The Crusades

Before concluding this chapter about the aftermath of Johannine anti-Judaism, I want to turn to the medieval period briefly. In 1095 CE, Pope Urban II addressed a church council that had been called in Clermont, in what is modern France. Just fifty years earlier, in 1054 CE, Western Christianity had formally separated from Eastern Byzantine Christianity; the reasons for the Great Schism were historically complex and had been brewing for centuries. But when Urban II addresses those gathered at Clermont, he calls for Christians in the West to take up a military campaign in the East ostensibly to protect fellow Christians from the conquests of Islam:

> As most of you have heard, the Turks and Arabs have attacked them and have conquered the territory of Romania [i.e., the Byzantine Empire] as far west as the shore of the Mediterranean and the Hellespont . . . They have killed and captured many, and have destroyed the churches and devastated the empire. . . . On this account I, or rather the Lord, beseech you as Christ's heralds to publish this everywhere and to persuade all people of whatever rank, foot-soldiers and knights, poor and rich, to carry aid promptly to those Christians and to destroy that vile race from the lands of our friends. . . . Christ commands it. All who die on the way, whether by land or by sea, or in battle against the pagans, shall have immediate remission of sins.[14]

In the decades and centuries following this speech crusader missions were launched from the West toward the East. Much has been written about this chapter in Christian history, for it helps us understand the fusion of religion and politics in the form of "holy war." The well-known historian of the Crusades, Steven Runciman, has called the campaigns "one long act of intolerance in the name of God."[15] Scripture, of course, could be mined in support of the war; so, too, could the long history of scriptural interpretation lend justification to the enterprise.

One important passage used in the early stages of the Crusades was the story of the "cleansing" of the Jerusalem Temple, especially the story as found in John, which, if you recall, is located in a unique position in this Gospel—not at the end of the Gospel and just preceding Jesus's trial and execution, but rather very nearly at the start of the Gospel, in chapter 2:

> The Passover of the Jews was near, and Jesus went up to Jerusalem. In the temple he found people selling cattle, sheep, and doves, and the money changers seated at their tables. Making a *whip of cords,* he drove all of them out of the temple, both the sheep and the cattle. He also poured out the coins of the money changers and overturned their tables. He told those who were selling doves, "Take these things out of here! Stop making my Father's house a marketplace!" (Jn 2:13–16, emphasis added)

John's Gospel is the only one that includes the story of Jesus making a "whip of cords"—a violent and potent image. The Greek word that John uses for "whip" (*fragellion*) is used only once in the New Testament, here in John, but its related verbal form ("to flog") was used to describe particularly violent punishments of criminals and slaves; it is also used to describe Jesus's flogging during his trial (Mark 15:15). Although early interpreters minimized the violence of John's account of Jesus driving out the moneychangers, or even sought to claim that Jesus could not have done what this story describes, the story was employed to distinguish between orthodox and heretical Christians. Augustine, for example, justified violence against heretics on the basis of the story—the "whip" and Jesus's "whippings" should be read quite literally, he argued.[16]

According to historian Katherine Smith, the eleventh and twelfth centuries saw a renewed interest in the Temple narrative in John 2, especially to support the crusader campaigns:

> In the decades following 1099, as the First Crusade's historiography took shape, growing Christian anxieties about the monetary economy were being displaced onto Jews, as part of a process whereby Jewish moneylending was linked to avarice, idolatry, carnality and pollution. The cleansing of the Temple was a natural exegetical locus for these anxieties.[17]

The Temple in Jerusalem took on strangely paradoxical meanings during the Crusades, for it was no longer just a symbol but "a physical holy site in need of defense. . . . Some authors went so far as to identify the liberation of the Temple, alongside that of the Holy Sepulchre, as the original motivation for the First Crusade."[18] The Fourth Gospel's story of Jesus with his whip in the Temple came to be mapped onto a place such as Jerusalem and extended the hostility toward Jews now to Muslims, which "by transforming the userers and simoniacs of exegetical tradition into avaricious, idolatrous Muslims, added an original chapter to the corpus of Gospel commentary that stretched back to Late Antiquity."[19] As with John 8:44, the story of Jesus with his whip in the Temple could be used to justify violence against those deemed heretics, against Jews, and against Muslims—the mobilization of holy war rendered all opponents, including even fellow Christians, ripe for whipping, for domination, for execution.

During the sixteenth-century reform movements in Europe, the interpretation of John's account of Jesus in the Temple, driving out the money changers with a whip, will resurface—especially in the form of art. If one looks at depictions of the story during this period, one finds that nearly all of the representations show Jesus with a whip in hand—the whip that only appears in the

Fourth Gospel's account. Take, for example, one of the most famous depictions of the scene: the oil painting done by El Greco sometime during the sixteenth century and now housed in the National Gallery of Art in Washington, DC. Here you find an image of men, women, and children in a colonnaded building; many of them are partially clothed, with one woman clasping her chest and seated next to a cage full of white doves. The figures are all writhing and swaying beneath Jesus who wields a whip in his right hand. His hand is upraised in a violent gesture that suggests he is about to whip the group of people, perhaps the woman with the doves in particular. It's a striking image that depicts the story as told only in the Gospel of John. Another example can be found at the Metropolitan Museum in New York City: here a sixteenth-century engraving by Marcantonio Raimondi, who was indebted to the work of Albrecht Dürer, depicts Jesus with raised whip standing over a money changer lying on the floor.

Such images could be read in new ways over the course of time; in accord with changing circumstances and political expediencies, the story's meaning varied: it could be read as Jesus and "the Jews" in the Temple; Protestant reformers regard the story as an indictment against the papacy; and during the Counter-Reformation and in the wake of the Council of Trent it comes to be read as an accusation against Protestants who should be punished for their heresies.

Conclusion

According to Joshua Trachtenberg, "Christendom's hostility toward the Jew reached its apogee in the post-Crusade period."[20] There are many factors, of course, that led to Christian anti-Judaism, but one essential impetus was the language of the

FIGURE 4.1. "The Cleansing of the Temple," Marcantonio Raimondi after Albrecht Dürer. Credit: The Metropolitan Museum of Art, New York, public domain.

Gospels themselves and, especially, the Gospel of John. It's all too easy to explain away Johannine language about "the Jews." Does *hoi ioudaioi* refer to Judeans rather than Jews? Should the language be read symbolically? Were "the Jews" simply characters meant to foil Jesus's ministry? Is saying that the Gospel of John is anti-Jewish an overreach or a misreading of its language?

In my view, reckoning with the anti-Jewish perspective is absolutely fundamental to understanding the Fourth Gospel and its legacy. Although we might wish it away, the fact is that John 8:44, John's story of Jesus's "whip of cords" in the Temple, and, above all, the Gospel's repeated use of "the Jews" for those who question Jesus, are hostile to him, and demand his crucifixion have reverberated throughout history and have been used to vilify Jews to genocidal ends.

As we will see in the next chapter, the distinct language of the Fourth Gospel will have repercussions for understanding the ideas of Martin Luther, the music of Johann Sebastian Bach, and the history of both anti-Judaism and more recently antisemitism. Although "the Jews" of John sometimes came to be used for heretics, Muslims, and others of various kinds, what remains is the consistency of the language itself, which would have reminded readers time and time again of Christian antagonism toward Jews. The "fear of the Jews" found in the Gospel of John continues to impact our contemporary world.

5

"The Truth Will Make You Free"

THE FOURTH GOSPEL AND THE REFORMATION

THE 1989 film *The Radicals,* which tells the story of Michael Sattler, a Benedictine prior who became one of the radical Protestant reformers of the sixteenth century, has a scene near the beginning that goes like this: the bishop of the monastery where Sattler is a prior hands Michael Sattler a piece of paper on which is printed a single biblical verse, a verse from the Gospel of John: "You shall know the truth, and the truth shall set you free" (Jn 8:32). The bishop expresses grave concern that this passage has been printed on its own without any interpretation. Sattler looks at the paper, repeats the words, and seems both puzzled and intrigued. Much about this scene is imagined, of course—it is, after all, a film, and screenwriters have license to play with history. But the elements of the scene—the Gospel of John, a scriptural passage printed by a printing press, and the concern about scripture being read without a priest or bishop offering interpretation—provide a useful entry into the subject of this chapter: the role of the Gospel of John during the Protestant reforms of the sixteenth century. Protestant Reformers were in part able to disseminate their ideas through printing, and one of the most important contributions of Martin Luther and others was their call for a return to scriptures; scriptures were not just for priests, they argued, but for the average Christian, too, who needed to read them, hear them read, devote time to understanding them.

The Protestant Reformation was arguably the most consequential development in Christian history. The impetus to make reforms within the Catholic Church had begun earlier with figures like Erasmus, a Dutch scholar who critiqued what he saw as some of the Church's errors. But it was figures like Martin Luther, Ulrich Zwingli, John Calvin, Conrad Grebel, Michael Sattler, William Tyndale, John Jewel, Richard Hooker, and others who energized a movement of reform that led eventually to a formal separation from the Catholic Church. These movements were fueled and facilitated by the invention of the printing press a century earlier—surely the most impactful technological development in the history of the Bible. Johannes Gutenberg's fifteenth-century invention of the printing press made it possible for the first time "to multiply written words in infinite quantity and in identical copies."[1] Gutenberg became most famous for producing the first printed Bibles, copies of the Latin version of both Old and New Testaments. Reformers of the sixteenth century used the printing press to spread their ideas and, as the scene in the film suggests, to print tracts centered on biblical texts.

In this chapter, I turn to stories from the Fourth Gospel that profoundly shaped some of the controversies of the sixteenth century. But first we look at the figure of Martin Luther, who claimed that "John's Gospel is the one, fine, true, and chief gospel, and is far, far to be preferred over the other three and placed high above them."[2]

Martin Luther and the Gospel of John

Much has been written about Martin Luther, who was a Catholic priest at Erfurt in Germany, and later became a professor of biblical studies at Wittenberg. In 1517, after his growing concerns about the Catholic Church's reliance on the sale of indulgences—certificates that ensured salvation—he posted what is now known as his *Ninety-Five Theses* on the door of the church in Wittenberg: "Those who believe," he wrote, "that they can be certain of their salvation because they have indulgence letters will be eternally damned, together with their teachers."[3] Luther's *Ninety-Five Theses* are often regarded as the official start of the Protestant Reformation, although history suggests that the story is more complicated; one thing is certain, according to historian Richard Marius: "The Ninety-five Theses made Luther famous within a month after he wrote them. They were picked up (perhaps by someone in the court of Albrecht of Mainz), translated into German, and carried from town to town in a rush of printing and reprinting."[4]

By 1521, after becoming convinced that the ability to understand and read scripture was essential to Christian faith, Luther set about translating the Latin version of the Bible—long the official version used by the Roman Catholic Church—into German, a vernacular language, the language of the people. In the preface to his German translation of the New Testament, published in 1522, Luther asks, "Which are the true and noblest books of the New Testament?" His response is telling:

> John's Gospel and St. Paul's epistles, especially that to the Romans, and St. Peter's first epistle are the true kernel and marrow of all the books. They ought properly to be the foremost books, and it would be advisable for every Christian to

> read them first and most, and by daily reading to make them as much as his own as his daily bread. For in them you do not find many works and miracles of Christ described, but you do find depicted in masterly fashion how faith in Christ overcomes sin, death, and hell, and gives life, righteousness, and salvation. . . . Now John writes very little about the works of Christ, but very much about His preaching, while the other evangelists write much about His works and little about His preaching.[5]

Luther was not particularly interested in the stories of Jesus's miracles, in contrast to so much of what know about the spread of Christianity. Instead, Luther privileged the Gospel of John above the other Gospels because it contains such extensive passages of Jesus preaching and teaching.

It's difficult to imagine that Luther's ideas about Jews and Judaism were not both informed by and contributed to his elevation of the Gospel of John, whose anti-Jewish bias is so pronounced. In his brief treatise *That Jesus Christ Was Born a Jew,* published in 1523, he seemed to adopt a somewhat favorable view, based on a reading of the birth narratives of Jesus in Matthew and Luke, although part of his goal in this treatise is to suggest that "if one deals in a kindly way with the Jews and instructs them carefully from Holy Scripture, many of them will become genuine Christians and turn again to the faith of their fathers, the prophets and patriarchs."[6] It is typical of Luther's approach here to suggest that the Old Testament prophets and the patriarchs, such as Abraham, were Christians by faith; these ideas go back to the earliest centuries of Christianity. Already in the fourth century, Eusebius had suggested that the very first verse of John's Gospel was the teaching of Moses who wrote the story of creation and that only Christians follow Abraham's religion.[7] Luther's overarching message in *That Jesus Christ Was Born a Jew* was to encourage readers to "deal gently" with Jews so that they might convert to Christianity.

But nearly twenty years later, his 1542 treatise *On the Jews and Their Lies* is altogether different and it makes for troubling reading, for it shows "his prevailing hatred of the Jewish people."[8] In this treatise, he claims that the passage in John 4:22, where Jesus says to the Samaritan woman that "salvation is from the Jews," explains in part why Jews are boastful—the main argument of this treatise. "Jews will not give up their pride and boasting about their nobility and lineage," he writes, but they are "miserable, blind, and senseless" and "real liars and bloodhounds."[9] In his charges against Jews as liars, the influence of John 8:44 is unambiguous. For Luther, the Jews were the Antichrist.[10] Luther's bias against the Jews is not merely an intellectual position, for he suggests that violence is appropriate against Jews who do not convert to Christianity: "Burn their places of worship (Luther actually goes so far as to claim that the Hebrew Scriptures support this), destroy their homes, seize their prayer books and Talmudic writings, and, since they refuse to change their ways (i.e., convert), expel them."[11]

Luther's ideas about the importance of scripture and faith formed part of his theology of salvation, which can be summarized succinctly as *sola scriptura, sola fide, sola gratia, solus Christus*: only by scripture, faith, grace, and Christ is one saved. Luther mined the scriptures in support of this claim. One way to consider how the Gospel of John, in particular, became enmeshed with sixteenth-century debates within various branches of the Protestant reform movements is to examine a couple of Johannine stories and sayings that become mobilized in the service of reformation debates.

Baptism, Eucharist, and the Reformers

Already in Paul's letters, written in the 50s CE, we find explicit mention of two ritual practices among the followers of Jesus: baptism and the eucharist, also called the Lord's Supper. Over time, these two practices come to be seen as sacraments; the term "sacrament" comes from the Latin *sacramentum*, which was itself a translation of the Greek word for mystery (*mysterium*). Sacraments were seen as the way to partake in the mystery of Christ, and they were essential to Christian practice. The belief in the "Word made flesh" (Jn 1:14)—the Incarnation—was just one scriptural basis for sacraments like the practices of baptism and the eucharist. Among the references to the practice of baptism, such as those found in Paul and the Gospel of Matthew, Christian tradition also looked to passages like John 3:5 in support of baptism: "Jesus answered, 'Very truly, I tell you, no one can enter the kingdom of God without being born of water and Spirit.' " In the case of the eucharist, John 6, which we looked at briefly in chapter 3, became important for interpreting the practice, alongside the letters of Paul.

By and large, in the earliest centuries of Christian history, it was adults who were baptized: this is what we find in the stories contained in the New Testament itself and in the first catechetical texts of the second and third centuries. With Augustine, whose ideas about original sin were to have a lasting impact on the church, infant baptism began to become more normative and, eventually, became a doctrinal mandate. In addition to John 3:5, interpreters could look to the story of Jesus's own baptism, which has an unusual rendering of the scene when compared with the Synoptic Gospels. Matthew, Mark, and Luke make it quite explicit that Jesus is baptized by John the Baptist: "In those days Jesus came from Nazareth of Galilee and was baptized by John in the Jordan," as Mark puts it simply (Mk 1:9). The Gospel of John, however, seems deliberately to avoid saying that John the Baptist baptized Jesus:

> The next day he [i.e., John the Baptist] saw Jesus coming toward him and declared, "Here is the Lamb of God who takes away the sin of the world! This is he of whom I said, 'After me comes a man who ranks ahead of me because he was before me.' I myself did not know him; but I came baptizing with water for this reason, that he might be revealed to Israel." And John testified, "I saw the Spirit descending from heaven like a dove, and it remained on him. I myself did not know him, but the one who sent me to baptize with water said to me, 'He on whom you see the Spirit descend and remain is the one who baptizes with the Holy Spirit.'" (John 1:29–33)

There is an allusion perhaps to Jesus's baptism here, but it is indirect at best. John the Baptist simply speaks of seeing the spirit descending on him, the one he calls the Lamb of God. In part, the avoidance of a direct claim that John baptizes Jesus may be due to ancient ideas about baptism—a form of ritual cleansing in water—namely, that the one who is spiritually superior baptizes those who are inferior. The Fourth Gospel seems to be taking pains to avoid depicting this head-on the way that the Gospel of Mark does.

And then in chapter 3, we find the story of Nicodemus, where Jesus speaks of being born of "water and Spirit." These passages in the Fourth Gospel, along with the stories of baptism in the Book of Acts, take on new importance during the sixteenth century as fresh debates about the practice of baptism unfolded. What good is faith if what is required of a Christian is to be baptized? Should infants be baptized? What is the meaning of baptism as a practice? Anabaptist reformers derived their name from the Greek words *ana* and *baptizein,* which meant "re-baptize." The language here is evocative of John 3, where Nicodemus asks Jesus how one can be "born again" or "born from above" and Jesus responds by speaking of being born of water and Spirit. In a tract that Michael Sattler may have written, we find an explicit reference to John 3 on the meaning of baptism: "Christ baptized," the text reads, "all whom He had elected and endowed them with His Holy Spirit."[12] *The Schleitheim Confession,* written in 1527 by Anabaptists in response to other reform movements, is more explicit about who should be baptized and when:

> Baptism shall be given to all those who have learned repentance and amendment of life, and who believe truly that their sins are taken away by Christ, and to all those who walk in the resurrection of Jesus Christ, and wish to be buried with Him in death, so that they may be resurrected with Him, and to all those who with this significance request baptism of us and demand it for themselves. *This excludes all infant baptism, the highest and chief abomination of the pope.*[13]

For the Anabaptists, the requirement was intention, a conscious decision, to be baptized; this "excludes" baptisms of babies, who cannot make a deliberate conscious choice.

Alongside controversies about baptism, the meaning of the eucharist was also hotly debated during the Reformation. Here, too, was a sacrament that went back to the earliest stages of Christianity, and by the fifth century, the celebration of the eucharist—the word itself meant in Greek "thanksgiving"—was an essential part of the Christian Mass. Different meanings had been given to the practice from an early stage. The earliest account of the practice comes in the letters of Paul, principally in 1 Corinthians:

> For I received from the Lord what I also handed on to you, that the Lord Jesus on the night when he was betrayed took a loaf of bread, and when he had given thanks, he broke it and said, "This is my body that is for you. Do this in remembrance of me." In the same way he took the cup also, after supper, saying, "This cup is the new covenant in my blood. Do this, as often as you drink it, in remembrance of me." For as often as you eat this bread and drink the cup, you proclaim the Lord's death until he comes. (1 Cor 11:23–26)

Unlike the Synoptic Gospels, the Fourth Gospel alludes to the eucharist by way of an extended dialogue between Jesus and "the Jews," as we saw in the previous chapter. Here Jesus says "I am the bread of life," "I am the bread that came down from heaven," and "I am the living bread that came down from heaven. Whoever eats of this bread will live forever; and the bread that I will give for the life of the world is my flesh" (Jn 6:35, 41, 51). He goes on to claim that "unless you eat the flesh of the Son of Man and drink his blood, you have no life in you. Those who eat my flesh and drink my blood have eternal life, and I will raise them up on the last day" (Jn 6:53–54). Martin Luther, Ulrich Zwingli, and the Anabaptists drew upon such passages to articulate their claims about both the practice of the eucharist and its meaning. They likewise drew upon a passage beloved by Erasmus himself, which comes right on the heels of the dialogue: "It is the spirit that gives life; the flesh is useless. The words that I have spoken to you are spirit and life" (Jn 6:63).

Reformers like the Swiss Zwingli, a Catholic priest turned protestant preacher, were deeply opposed to Luther's ideas about the eucharist—namely the idea of consubstantiation, which said that in the eucharist the wine and the bread became the actual blood and body of Christ. Luther's sermons on the Gospel of John 6 suggest that "God is to be apprehended and found in the flesh and blood of Christ solely by faith. We must know that this flesh and blood, though real, not only have the qualities of flesh and blood but partake in the Divine."[14] In his sermons on the Gospel of John, Luther emphasizes time and again the importance of faith, and yet he continues to wrestle with the reality of both Jesus's flesh and blood, and the meaning of the eucharist. In his response to Luther, Zwingli writes in his *Commentary on True and False Religion*:

> We must, then, hold a different view of the flesh and blood of this sacrament from that which the theologians have thus far laid down, whose opinion is opposed by all sense and reason and understanding and by faith itself . . . Let us now see how finely these things fit together: by faith we believe that the bodily and sensible flesh of Christ is here present. . . . Observe, therefore, what a monstrosity of speech this is: I believe that I eat the sensible and bodily flesh. For if it is bodily, there is no need of faith, for it is perceived by sense; and things perceived by sense have no need of faith.[15]

Here Zwingli is opposing the idea that during the Eucharist, Christians "eat the sensible and bodily flesh." Rather, he argues for the importance of the *symbolic* nature of the eucharist and of Jesus's claims about his own identity in the Gospel of John. When Jesus says that he is the "way" or the "vine" or the "light" (Jn 14:6, 15:5, 8:12), he does not mean this *literally* but rather symbolically or metaphorically. Is Jesus actually a Lamb, Zwingli asks on the basis of Jn 1:36? Absolutely not. The language of the Fourth Gospel, the language of the eucharist, must be understood symbolically and spiritually.

Bach's *St. John Passion*

I began this book with Johann Sebastian Bach's *St. John Passion* and the opposition to its continued performance today. It is fitting to return to it here, because it offers us a vivid aural example of what happens to the Gospel of John during and in the wake of the Reformation. Bach, a devoted follower of Luther, composed the orchestral and choral piece soon after he took up the position as Cantor at the St. Thomas Church in Leipzig. It was first performed on Good Friday in 1724 in Leipzig's St. Nicholas Church, which was built in the twelfth century as a Catholic Church but in the seventeenth century became Protestant. Bach's choral and orchestral work, according to Michael Marissen, "is an extended musical commentary on and interpretation of John."[16] A few features of the work stand out immediately: first, the text is in German, not in Latin. This is significant when we recall that one of Luther's key contributions in the first half of the sixteenth century was to prepare a German translation of the Bible. We should not underestimate the controversies caused by a translation to the vernacular and Bach's use of the German language is significant (and entirely different from, say, his *Mass in b minor*, which was in Latin). We can also note the incorporation of chorales, which in part were influenced by Luther's own compositions of hymns to be sung by congregations (rather than a Mass to be chanted by a choir or officiants); for Luther, music was a language of God, much like the scriptures. The Gospel, he argued, could be preached through song.

To some extent what we can hear in the *St. John Passion* is a kind of historical layering: we've looked at the language of the Gospel of John itself, turned to the way the language about "the Jews" comes to be inflected during the Crusades and now, in this chapter, seen what happens to Christian theology and ideology during the Reformation. It would be an oversimplification to argue that Bach simply borrows Luther's anti-Jewish ideology, but Dagmar Hoffmann-Axhelm has suggested that the structure Bach chose for the work—including repetitions of biblical passages—served as a "biblically sanctioned and thus religiously constituted, Luther-bolstered and textually and musically integrated hostility towards Jews."[17] From the ominous opening of the work—what Martin Geck has called "a vocal and instrumental tone-painting of hitherto unprecedented power in the history of Western music"—to the closing resolution of the final chorale, the work serves to both interpret and heighten Johannine language.[18]

Let's look at some of the libretto, the text, which Bach drew both from the Gospel and from previous librettists, to see how the piece uses the Gospel of John. In what follows, it's important to keep in mind that the character of the "Evangelist" is the narrator of John's Gospel: by tradition, the Evangelist John. The chorus plays the role of the crowds, the people, and more specifically, "the Jews." The focus of the piece is on John 18–19, the lectionary reading for Good Friday. It begins with 18:1–8, which describes Jesus going with his disciples to a garden in the Kidron valley, where Judas brings soldiers who are looking for Jesus and begins with the evangelist's (i.e., John's) narrative:

> EVANGELIST: Jesus went with his disciples across the brook Kidron, where there was a garden, where Jesus and his disciples went in. Judas, however, who betrayed him, also knew the spot, for Jesus often gathered in that place with his disciples. Now when Judas had engaged the band and attendants of the chief priests and of the Pharisees, he comes there with torches, lanterns, and

with weapons. Now as Jesus knew everything that should happen to him, he went out and declares to them:

JESUS: Whom do you seek?

EVANGELIST: They answered him:

CHORUS: Jesus of Nazareth.

EVANGELIST: Jesus declares to them:

JESUS: I am the one.

EVANGELIST: Judas, however, who betrayed him, also stood with them. Now since Jesus declared to them that "I am the one," they drew back and fell to the ground. He then asked them once more:

JESUS: Whom do you seek?

EVANGELIST: They again exclaimed:

CHORUS: Jesus of Nazareth.

EVANGELIST: Jesus answered:

JESUS: I have said this to you that it is I; for if you are in fact looking for me, then let these others go![19]

Look at how the oral choreography here works as a distinctive dialogue among three characters: the narrator of John's Gospel, the chorus, and Jesus. It is a dramatic rendering of what might seem like a simple quotation from John 18. The role of the Evangelist (i.e., John), sung by a tenor, provides the narrative in recitative form—a kind of musical speech—taken from the Fourth Gospel. The character of Jesus is sung by a bass singer, who seems both serene and authoritative. The chorus is insistent and the music reflects that rhythmically. The musicologist Wilfrid Mellers describes this opening chorus like this: "The four bars of fast music have a bass of rocking thirds, chattering figuration in semiquavers for flutes and violins, and briskly metrical homophony for the voices, yapping for Christ's blood."[20]

Interspersed throughout the piece there are chorales—distinct from the chorus, which recites from John. These chorales can sometimes seem like a reprieve from the text of John; they draw from the language of John, at times, but are quite distinct. They are written in four-part harmony, the melodies are lyrical, and they draw heavily from congregational singing. Indeed, many of them continue to be sung as hymns by various Christian denominations.

Throughout the work, each character—Jesus, Pilate, Peter—recreates the dialogue from the trial and execution scenes. Crucially, for our purposes, the chorus appears specifically as "the Jews," who demand ever more insistently that Pilate find Jesus guilty; Pilate seems hesitant and resigned. The tension mounts until it reaches a climax with "the Jews" calling for his crucifixion:

EVANGELIST: And the soldiers plaited a crown of thorns, and put it upon his head, and put on him a purple robe, and said exclaimed:

CHORUS: Greetings, dear King of the Jews.

EVANGELIST: And gave him blows to the face. Then Pilate went back out and exclaimed to them:

PILATE: Behold, I am leading him out to you, so that you will recognize that I find no guilt in him.

EVANGELIST: Thus Jesus went out, wearing a crown of thorns, and the purple robe, and [Pilate] exclaimed to them:

PILATE: Behold, what a man!

EVANGELIST: When the chief priests and attendants beheld him, they shouted out and exclaimed:

CHORUS: Crucify, crucify!

EVANGELIST: Pilate exclaimed to them:

PILATE: Take him away and crucify him; for I find no guilt in him!

EVANGELIST: The Jews answered him:

CHORUS: We have a law, and according to the law he ought to die: for he has made himself the Son of God. . . .

EVANGELIST: From this, henceforth, Pilate sought how he might release him. . . . But the Jews shouted out and exclaimed:

CHORUS: If you release this one, then you are no friend of the emperor's; for whoever makes himself a king is against the emperor.

EVANGELIST: When Pilate heard those words, he led Jesus out and sat himself on the judgment seat, at the place that is called "High Pavement," but "Gabbatha" in Hebrew. It was, however, the preparation day in Passover, at the sixth hour, and he [Pilate] exclaims to the Jews:

PILATE: Behold this is your King!

EVANGELIST: But they shouted out:

CHORUS: Away, away with him, crucify him!

It is the insistence of the crowd, "the Jews," who shout for Jesus to be put to death, that makes this interpretation of the Gospel of John so vivid and dramatic. Bach has heightened the tension of John's text with the music itself: Pilate sounds more and more reluctant, more resigned and almost sorrowful; "the Jews" clamor for Jesus's crucifixion with rhythmic chants, striking an almost militaristic tone. Mellers notes that "the music is at once savage and ritualized," though he problematically adds, "as crowds often are."[21] It is not simply that John deploys *crowds* to oppose Jesus, it is that the language of John, Luther, and Bach (and many others) conveys a Jesus opposed specifically to "the Jews." Words matter, then and now.

Conclusion

To some extent what we hear in Bach's *St. John Passion* reveals a culminative affect of the Fourth Gospel's afterlives: we've looked at the language of the Gospel of John itself, turned to the way the language about "the Jews" comes to be inflected during the Crusades and now, in this chapter, what happens to Christian theology and ideology during the Reformation. It would be an oversimplification to argue that Bach simply borrows Luther's anti-Jewish ideology, but the reverberations of Johannine ideas and language are unmistakable more than sixteen hundred years after the Gospel was written. From the ominous opening of the *St. John Passion* to the closing resolution of the final chorale, the work serves to both interpret and heighten what had already become Christian tradition: the soaring language of the Fourth Gospel was rich in meaning; the plot of the Gospel and its characters told a violent story; the truths of the Gospel served to divide Christians from their others, especially "the Jews."

The controversies about modern performances of the work will no doubt continue. Ruth HaCohen has described one particular performance that sought to "mitigate the questionable import of the *St. John Passion*": "On Good Friday of 2005 in Stuttgart," she writes, "in a gesture prompted by the desire to broaden and contemporize the oratorical appeal of the *St. John Passion*, the aria texts were successfully superseded by Jewish, Muslim, and nonreligious equivalents, communicated kindred spiritual-emotional messages."[22] Substituting alternative texts suggests again just how much words matter; the words that the Gospel of John uses are not merely symbolic or abstract: they are born of a particular time in history, yes, but their afterlives persistently resound across time and place. And thinking through the resonances of musical adaptations of the Fourth Gospel allows us to expand our understanding of its sensory legacies.

6

"You Must Be Born Again"

JOHN'S GOSPEL AMONG AMERICAN EVANGELICALS AND BEYOND

IN 1971, at the edge of "Slab City," California, Leonard Knight built what has come to be called Salvation Mountain. Knight was a self-proclaimed born-again Pentecostal, a movement that began in the early twentieth century and was inspired by the story of the disciples gathered in Jerusalem after Jesus's death and resurrection in the Book of Acts: "All of them were filled with the Holy Spirit and began to speak in other languages, as the Spirit gave them ability" (Acts 2:4). Being "filled with the Holy Spirit" is the experiential goal of Pentecostalism. In the vein of early Christian ascetics who left cities for desert solitude, Knight wanted to create "a mountain to honor his God and to share his faith with others."[1] The colorfully painted mountain is inscribed with biblical verses: at the top is inscribed "God is love," which comes from Johannine literature: "God is love, and those who abide in love abide in God, and God abides in them" (1 John 4:16). At the center of the mountain is an inscription alluding to the words and ideas from the Book of Acts important to Pentecostal theology. And just to the left of the

FIGURE 6.1. “Salvation Mountain,” Slab City, California. Credit: The Jon B. Lovelace Collection of California Photographs in Carol M. Highsmith’s America Project, Library of Congress, Prints and Photographs Division.

central heart image, is the verse, John 3:16: “For God so loved the world that he gave his only Son, so that everyone who believes in him may not perish but may have eternal life.”

The mountain can be read as a kind of monumental artwork or large-scale sculpture with its vivid colors and constructed rise set against the surrounding desert landscape; it stands both as a testimony to Knight’s faith and also functions now as a pilgrimage destination. And it offers us yet another medium through which to understand John’s legacy.

Knight’s theology drew heavily from Pentecostal ideas of the Spirit and a baptism by fire, and here on salvation mountain he demonstrated his indebtedness to Johannine passages and ideas. The Fourth Gospel, too, has an interest in the “Holy Spirit” and contains another a term important to Knight—namely, “Advocate”:

> But the Advocate, the Holy Spirit, whom the Father will send in my name, will teach you everything, and remind you of all that I have said to you. (14:26)
>
> When the Advocate comes, whom I will send to you from the Father, even the Spirit of truth who comes from the Father; he will testify on my behalf. (15:26)
>
> Nevertheless I tell you the truth: it is to your advantage that I go away, for if I do not go away, the Advocate will not come to you; but if I go, I will send him to you. (16:7)

All of these verses are connected by way of the term "Advocate," also frequently rendered as "Counselor." The word is a translation of the Greek word *paraklētos,* which meant a "helper," an "assistant," or a "comforter." Studies have shown that one of the main ways that the Bible is used in contemporary American life is as a "comfort," and the idea of an advocate, someone who comes to your aid, as found in the Fourth Gospel serves this use well. But Slab City is also an example of an experiential approach to the Bible—visitors move around the hill, take in the colors, read the texts—in part in opposition to an intellectual approach, as Sara Patterson suggests:

> Just as nineteenth-century Baptists and Methodists and twentieth-century Pentecostal and Holiness believers did, Knight placed emphasis on *experience* over education as the site of religious authority. This is most evident in the way he described himself; he often referred to himself as stupid and silly, thus simultaneously reinforcing God's power and his own experiential authority.[2]

Knight's mountain is a visual entry into the themes of this chapter, which turns to several forms of distinctly American Christianity—the Mormons, Jehovah's Witnesses, and Pentecostals—to unpack the ways these traditions have drawn upon the themes of the Fourth Gospel. These forms of Christianity have now, of course, spread throughout the world, in part because each of them emphasize the importance of mission work and proselytizing.

Two caveats are important at the outset: first, we only have space to touch a few key aspects of these traditions that illuminate John's legacy; second, I want to be cautious about my use of the term "evangelical," as it appears in the title of this chapter. We will unpack this term briefly in this chapter, but it is worth noting that among scholars of American religious history there is substantial debate about the extent to which the term remains useful. Matthew Sutton has argued most recently that we should not use the term as a catch-all for movements that "affirmed a specific set of abstract theological ideas" derived at least in part from scripture.[3] Not all of the groups I discuss in this chapter would fall neatly into any definition of "evangelical," but we are on firmer ground when we turn to our starting point: the sermons of Billy Graham and the distillation of the Christian message within a single biblical verse, John 3:16.

An Evangelical Mantra

If contemporary American "evangelical" Christianity could be reduced to one biblical verse, it might well be John 3:16, quoted in full on Salvation Mountain. In Good News Bible schools and "Jesus Camps," evangelical megachurches and charismatic sermons, this verse is one that is rehearsed, memorized, instilled. Folks place signs with John 3:16 on them in their yards, affix them to trees in their fields, and post them along the edges of roads to catch the eyes of drivers. A quick search on Amazon reveals over 20,000 items with John 3:16 written on them, including t-shirts, hats, bracelets, wall-decorations, crosses, sweatshirts, stickers, American flags, bookmarks, pens, license plate frames, key chains, swimming trunks, throw pillows, embossed wallets, and more. In accord with the season, new items are added frequently: John 3:16 heart-shaped stress balls, for example, in time for Valentine's Day. Most recently, the non-profit advertising entity "He Gets Us" televised one of their ads during the first half of the 2025 Super Bowl; in one frame we see an individual wearing a baseball cap backward and on the cap: John 3:16. Just the reference to the verse is sufficient on all of these examples; paraphernalia does not need to include actual words of the verse because it is so widely known.

The evangelical preacher Billy Graham, in one of his 1977 sermons, called John 3:16 "the most familiar passage in all the Bible," "the Bible in a nutshell," and "the Gospel in miniature."[4] In the 1970s and 80s, Rollen Fredrick Stewart—who went by the name Rainbow Man because he wore a rainbow afro-style wig—was a regular fixture at American sporting events where he held up signs reading John 3:16. The American football player Tim Tebow began inscribing biblical citations on his black under-eye strips before games, most famously using John 3:16, about which he said: "Because as a Christian, that's the essence of our Christianity, it's the essence of our hope." One of country music singer Keith Urban's songs has the title and chorus: "John Cougar, John Deere, and John 3:16." In the recent television show *The Righteous Gemstones,* one individual becomes a preacher of a church simply on the basis of his ability to quote John 3:16. Street art, graffiti, and wall murals, including some found on central town squares just opposite courthouses, cite the verse, often with an image of the crucifixion.

In the digital realm, the website www.topverses.com ranks the mostly widely cited top verses from the Bible and leading the rankings is John 3:16, followed by John 1:1 and John 14:6.

About the website topverses.com, Bryan Bibb has written: "One suspects that the Top Verses algorithm presents a fairly clear picture of what average readers think the Bible is and is about. In this view, the Bible is a collection of verses to give people hope and encouragement, to tell people about the coming of Jesus the Messiah, and to make sure we know that Jesus is the only way to salvation."[5] In looking at the favorite Bible verses list, John 3:16 ranks second only to Psalm 23 ("The Lord is my shepherd"). The list of the contemporary lives of John 3:16 could go on.

The verse carries a simultaneous message of love ("God so loved the world") and salvation—those "who believe" will have "eternal life"—and a message of exclusion, intolerance, and a single-minded focus on belief. Through its memorization, John 3:16 fosters a collective sense of insider subjectivity. The legacy of this verse is a springboard to understanding more broadly how modern American evangelical movements have drawn upon the language and ideology of John to cultivate community and to construct strict borders around Christian identity. The place to begin is with the Fourth Gospel's story of Nicodemus, where the verse is found. It's a story that is unique to John, and one that has a rich and complex afterlife.

The Story of Nicodemus

In chapter 3, we looked at the way the gnostics drew on the Gospel of John and how the language of above/below as found in the story of Nicodemus and throughout the Gospel suited their cosmology and Christology. Here I want to return to the story of Nicodemus in John 3, for it contains passages that are the backbone, the core, of evangelical theology. The story begins like this:

> Now there was a Pharisee named Nicodemus, a leader of the Jews. He came to Jesus by night and said to him, "Rabbi, we know that you are a teacher who has come from God; for no one can do these signs that you do apart from the presence of God." Jesus answered him, "Very truly, I tell you, no one can see the kingdom of God without being born *from above*." Nicodemus said to him, "How can anyone be born after having grown old? Can one enter a second time into the mother's womb and be born?" Jesus answered, "Very truly, I tell you, no one can enter the kingdom of God without being born of water and spirit. What is born of the flesh is flesh, and what is born of the Spirit is spirit. Do not be astonished that I said to you, 'You must be born *from above*.' " (Jn 3:1–3, emphasis added)

Here I want to pause to look at one particular word—the Greek word *anōthen,* which the New Revised Standard Version renders as "from above." The translation "from above" is both a more literal reading of the Greek and it accords well with Johannine language and imagery, which has a vertical (above and below) Christology, as we have already seen.

The King James Version of the Bible, still the most widely used version used in America, reads: "Jesus answered and said unto him, Verily, verily, I say unto thee, except a man be *born again,* he cannot see the kingdom of God." The New International Version, the translation favored and used by evangelicals in America, reads: "Jesus replied, 'Very truly I tell you, no one can see the kingdom of God unless they are *born again*'" (Jn 3:3). The NIV, published by an evangelical press (Zondervan), has developed into an industry of related publications, all of which include the translation of "born again."[6] The translation "you must be born again" is the one most familiar to American

Christians, and it lies at the heart of evangelical and fundamentalist Christianity, which holds that a person "must be born again" to have eternal life. The idea of regeneration captured in this particular verse appears in one of nineteenth-century evangelist Dwight Lyman Moody's sermons, which claims that being "born again" is not about going to church or childhood confirmation, but a complete transformation: a born-again person is "translated into new life, taken out of the power of darkness, and translated into the Kingdom of Light."[7]

As the story continues, Jesus instructs Nicodemus further about "heavenly things":

> No one has ascended into heaven except the one who descended from heaven, the Son of Man. And just as Moses lifted up the serpent in the wilderness, so must the Son of Man be lifted up, that whoever believes in him may have eternal life. For God so loved the world that he gave his only Son, so that everyone who believes in him may not perish but may have eternal life. Indeed, God did not send the Son into the world to condemn the world, but in order that the world might be saved through him. (Jn 3:13–17)

In one of the very earliest accounts of the Christian practice of baptism after the Gospel of John was written, the second-century apologist Justin Martyr describes the practice of baptism and specifically draws upon the "born again" language: after a period of fasting, he says, those ready for baptism,

> are brought by us where there is water, and are regenerated in the same manner in which we were ourselves regenerated. For, in the name of God, the Father and Lord of the universe, and of our Savior Jesus Christ, and of the Holy Spirit, they then receive the washing with water. For Christ also said,

> "Except ye be born again, ye shall not enter into the kingdom of heaven." Now, that it is impossible for those who have once been born to enter into their mothers' wombs, is manifest to all. (Justin, *Apology* 1.61)

If you look closely, Justin is implying that the passage—a story only found in John—is one that is brought to bear on the practice of Christian baptism. He also hints at the concerns that have already arisen about the meaning of the passage. Nicodemus himself does not understand Jesus; so, too, subsequent readers found the passage confusing. How would one have a second birth? During the Reformation, especially among Anabaptists, the phrase took on heightened meaning as they re-baptized those that had been baptized as infants. But in the second century, the questions about this verse seem to be much more literal.

"Born again" language is so ubiquitous in American evangelical Christianity that people often simply refer to evangelicals as "born-again Christians." Evangelical is a term with a wide application: if you recall, reformers in the sixteenth century were called evangelicals because they emphasized engaging closely with scripture. So, too, in the American context, the term can refer to Christian denominations from across the social and political spectrum, left-wing liberals and right-wing conservatives alike. This is even more the case with the use of the term globally. Any Protestant church that emphasizes the authority of scripture and the close attention to reading the scriptures, could be called evangelical. The term is often confused with "Fundamentalism," and indeed there some important overlaps between the two terms.[8] Fundamentalism emerged in the revival movements of the nineteenth century and solidified at a conference in 1895 with five points of "fundamentalism"; the first of these is the inerrancy of scripture: scripture is to be read literally, it does not contain errors, and as the word of God it has absolute authority. The importance of proselytizing—evangelizing, spreading the "good news"—runs throughout all of these movements.

Foot-Washing

One of the Christian practices that has its origin in the Gospel of John is foot-washing, known as "pedilavium" in Latin. It is a practice that has seen renewed interest among American evangelicals. As early as the third century, we find church writers suggesting that this should be done prior to the Eucharist. In the late ancient and medieval period, the practice comes to be part of the observance of Maundy Thursday, the Thursday prior to Easter. Here is the story as found in the Fourth Gospel:

> Now before the festival of the Passover, Jesus knew that his hour had come to depart from this world and go to the Father. Having loved his own who were in the world, he loved them to the end. The devil had already put it into the heart of Judas son of Simon Iscariot to betray him. And during supper Jesus, knowing that the Father had given all things into his hands, and that he had come from God and was going to God, got up from the table, took off his outer robe, and tied a towel around himself. Then he poured water into a basin and began to wash the disciples' feet and to wipe them with the towel that was tied around him. He came to Simon Peter, who said to him, "Lord, are you going to wash my feet?" Jesus answered, "You do not know now what I am doing, but later you will understand." Peter said to him, "You will never wash my feet." Jesus answered, "Unless I wash you, you have no share with me." Simon Peter said to him, "Lord,

> not my feet only but also my hands and my head!" Jesus said to him, "One who has bathed does not need to wash, except for the feet, but is entirely clean. And you are clean though not all of you." For he knew who was to betray him; for this reason he said, "Not all of you are clean." After he had washed their feet, had put on his robe, and had returned to the table . . . (Jn 13:1–13)

Christians have, throughout history, interpreted this passage differently, but many denominations and forms of Christianity have taken up the practice of a ritual foot-washing in religious services. In addition to the earliest examples from Roman Catholicism and the Greek Orthodox church, where priests washed the feet of laypersons, various Protestant groups like the Anabaptists, Lutherans, Anglicans, Methodists, Presbyterians, and Pentecostals incorporate the ritual of congregants washing each other's feet.

Mormons

In 1833, Joseph Smith, the founder of the Church of Jesus Christ of Latter-day Saints, also known as the Mormons, began the practice of foot-washing among his followers. According to one of his biographers, Richard Bushman, Smith "had washed the feet of thirteen brethren, following the example of Jesus in the Gospel of John. In 1836, a new kind of washing, one for the whole body, was instituted, following Old Testament Practices."[9] This is just one example of the ways that Smith, and subsequently the Mormons, looked to the Gospel of John. Nicholas Frederick has written of Joseph Smith:

> When studied closely, it becomes clear that Joseph Smith did not simply study the Bible; he interacted with it. He mingled

> his words and ideas with texts written nearly two millennia ago, believing that these writings were not necessarily solidified and sanctified by time and tradition. It appears quite likely that Joseph understood his literary and theological achievements to function as an "inspired explication" of texts both past and present. With the possible exception of the writings of Isaiah, nowhere does this "inspired explication" come out more fully than in Joseph Smith's use of the Gospel of John.[10]

Smith's close reading of the Gospel of John had begun some years prior as he was translating the Bible from the King James Version in an effort to "restore truths," which "clarified doctrine and improved scriptural understanding." According to the official Church of Jesus Christ of Latter-Day Saints, the translation is unlike others, because "Joseph's translation was more revelation than literal translation from one language into another."[11]

An excellent example of how Smith interpreted John can be seen in his translation of the opening of the Gospel:

> In the beginning was the gospel preached through the Son. And the gospel was the word, and the word was with the Son, and the Son was with God, and the Son was of God. The same was in the beginning with God. All things were made by him; and without him was not anything made which was made. In him was the gospel, and the gospel was the life, and the life was the light of men; and the light shineth in the world, and the world perceiveth it not. (Jn 1:1–5)[12]

Note how carefully this translation has shifted key elements of the prologue: here, what is first is the gospel, which is preached through the Son; it's the gospel that was the word, not the Son. This example shows that Smith, and subsequently his followers, did not believe in the inerrancy of scripture; no, they argued, the scriptures were written by humans and therefore they could have mistakes. Smith's revelations were necessary in part because they showed him where the scriptures were in need of correction.

In addition to the Bible and the *Book of Mormon,* the Mormon scriptures also include a work called *Doctrines and Covenants,* which include some extensive engagements with the Gospel of John. In *Doctrines and Covenants,* Smith rewrites the opening of the Gospel of John again, a rewriting that Frederick argues produces "an unknown version of the Gospel of John."[13] In this version, he changes the third person to first person—for example, "I saw his glory, that he was in the beginning"; "I, John, bear record that I beheld his glory, as the glory of the Only Begotten of the Father, full of grace and truth." As we have seen with other interpreters of the Gospel of John (and the Bible more generally): "Not content with simply studying John's Gospel, Joseph aspires to rewrite it, restoring to antiquity what he senses to be the truth of the present. He studies the ancient world not only to learn from it but also to correct it."[14]

In *Doctrines and Covenants,* Joseph Smith describes a vision he and Sidney Rygdon had while working on a translation of John 5:29, which says the dead "will hear [the Son of God's] voice and will come out, those who have done good, to the resurrection of life, and those who have done evil, to the resurrection of condemnation." Smith translates the passage: "And shall come forth; they who have done good, in the resurrection of the just; and they who have done evil, in the resurrection of the unjust" (D&C 76:17). What follows is a vision of "the glory of the Son, on the right hand of the Father . . . the holy angels, and them who are sanctified before his throne, worshipping God, and the Lamb, who worship him forever and ever" (D&C 76:20–21). It is one example, among many, of how the Mormon Church would come to understand the importance of Smith's revelations; it is his revelations that led him to a new understanding of the Gospel of John. *The Book of Mormon* itself purports to be the scriptures revealed to Smith, who also argued that it was essential to spread the truth through missions and, as of this writing, they have nearly 100,000 missionaries around the world.

Jehovah's Witnesses

Another mission-focused movement, the Jehovah's Witnesses—formally known as the Watch Tower Bible and Tract Society—also began in the nineteenth century, with the work of a preacher named C. T. Russell. The movement was based both on the importance of Bible study and the expectation of the coming Battle of Armageddon. Although Armageddon—a phonetic rendering of Har Megiddo, mount Megiddo—only appears in the Book of Revelation where it is the place of the end-times battle, it's worth remembering that indirectly this is connected to the Gospel of John since Christian *tradition* has frequently associated the John of the Fourth Gospel with the John of Revelation.

Jehovah's Witnesses are well known for their tracts that depict a multi-racial community of believers. One feature they extract from the Gospel of John seems to be its emphasis on love: "As you read the Gospel of John," their introduction to the Fourth Gospel says, "note Jesus's love for mankind, his humility, and his identity as the Messiah, the King of God's Kingdom"; and it is true that John's Gospel uses the word "love" far more than any other Gospel; indeed, it is second in frequency to the Book of Psalms in the entire Bible. Jehovah's Witnesses emphasize God's love for Jesus, the Son (e.g., Jn 3:35, 5:20; 10:17), Jesus's love for others (e.g., Jn 13:1), those who love Jesus (e.g., 14:21), and Jesus's call to "love one another" (Jn 13:34). It may seem strange that they draw on a theme of love, given that Jehovah's Witnesses continue to encourage singleness. Russell, after all, "regarded [sex] as more animalistic than spiritual," according to James Penton.[15]

One of the things Jehovah's Witnesses are best known for is their translation of the Bible, which was meant to be "a so-called 'literal translation' based largely on Rudolph Kittel's Biblia Hebraica and the Greek text of Westcott and Hort."[16] This in itself is striking, for Kittel's 1902 edition of the Hebrew Bible and Westcott and Hort's 1881 edition of the Greek New Testament were both prepared as critical editions, taking into account variants among the many manuscripts available. In their tracts, Jehovah's Witnesses emphasize the truth of the Bible: John 3:16, for example, shows that "God cares so deeply about us that he has gone to great lengths to make the fulfillment of his purpose a certainty."[17] We catch a glimpse of their theology and unique translation of John's opening in their *New World Translation*: "In the beginning was the word, and the Word was with God, and the Word was a god," which they gloss as the "Word was divine" or "a godlike one." They claim that "there are good reasons for saying that John did not mean that 'the Word' was the same as Almighty God."[18] The reasons they give for the Word not being the same as God are striking: they turn to the Greek text itself to make the case; and they draw attention to ancient versions of the text: "while the New World translation 'a god' is jarring in a contemporary setting," writes Penton, "the concept behind it has more support grammatically and historically than is generally recognized."[19] This is a kind of historical biblical criticism in the service of a theological message—namely, that Jesus was god-like but not precisely equal to God.

Pentecostals

The Pentecostal Movement, founded around 1900, drew its inspiration from the Book of Acts, but it was also inspired by the Gospel of John, as we've seen with the example of Knight's Salvation Mountain. The movement emphasizes the importance of the Holy Spirit and a baptism of the Spirit, and their worship services are known for glossolalia (speaking in tongues) and charismatic spontaneity. Above all, being "in the Spirit" is central, and here the story of Nicodemus becomes a prooftext because this is where Jesus says, "Very truly, I tell you, no one can enter the kingdom of God without being born of water and Spirit. What is born of the flesh is flesh, and what is born of the Spirit is spirit" (Jn 3:5). But the following Johannine passages, too, become important for the Pentecostal movement:

> God is spirit, and those who worship him must worship in spirit and truth. (Jn 4:24)
>
> It is the spirit that gives life; the flesh is useless. The words that I have spoken to you are spirit and life. (Jn 6:63)
>
> Now he said this about the Spirit, which believers in him were to receive, for as yet there was no Spirit because Jesus was not yet glorified. (Jn 7:39)
>
> But the Advocate, the Holy Spirit, whom the Father will send in my name, will teach you everything and remind you of all that I have said to you. (Jn 14:26)
>
> When he had said this, he breathed on them and said to them, "Receive the Holy Spirit." (Jn 20:22)

The 1997 film *The Apostle* depicts a Pentecostal preacher played by Robert Duvall. One of terms he uses repeatedly is the "Holy Ghost": "I'm a genuine, Holy Ghost, Jesus-filled preachin' machine this mornin'!"; "Holy Ghost Power"; "we got Holy Ghost power in this tent." The emotional and ecstatic forms of worship depicted in the film, including speaking in tongues, offers a cinematic rendering of Pentecostal services. Being filled with the Spirit is the basis and goal of worship, and here, the spirit language of the Fourth Gospel becomes particularly amplified.

It is worth noting that Pentacostalism takes us well beyond the American context. The American landscape of evangelism with its forms of Christianity bent on missionizing have now spread globally. The largest church in the world—the Yoido Full Gospel Church in South Korea—is a Pentecostal church; it attracts a *quarter of a million* attendees each Sunday. The First Love Church in Ghana draws from Pentecostal practices; its website also emphasizes the Gospel of John. Who is Jesus, they ask? It can be summed up in the idea of love taken from John: "This is my commandment, that you love one another as I have loved you. No one has greater love than this, to lay down one's life for one's friends" (Jn 15:12–13). Other African megachurches in South Africa and Nigeria are Pentecostal in their orientation, as are megachurches found in South America. Pentecostalism is the fastest growing form of Christianity and although there are now many different denominations that are Pentecostal, the fundamental mission remains: a baptism of the Spirit, expressed so explicitly by the story of Nicodemus in the Gospel of John.

As we consider the legacy of John in the global context, one of the many complexities that emerges is the frequently tense relationship between religion and politics. According to historian Mark Noll, diverse understandings of "the word of God," a phrase that owes much to the opening of the Gospel of John, existed from "the beginning of European-American history": "The Bible of Christendom arrived in the New World as the Scripture of state-church Christianity, even as the spaciousness of that world opened up room for Bible-believers opposed to Christendom."[20] The Gospel of John was written at a time when religion and politics were entirely interwoven, and in spite of an American so-called separation of church and state, history continues to reveal how encounters with biblical texts bridge these imagined distinctions.

Billboard Evangelism

Drive the highways of the United States and it's likely you will find passages from the Gospel of John on billboards. Particularly ubiquitous additions to the billboard array are those that were installed by Christian Aid Ministries. Founded by Anabaptists, the nonprofit "strives to be an honest, efficient channel enabling the church to minister to physical and spiritual needs around the world."[21] Although the group began by doing humanitarian work and Bible distribution in eastern Europe, it expanded its mission in 2006 with billboards across the United States. The billboards usually feature a prominent and sensational statement, a phone number to call for more information, and a reference to a passage from the Bible. Statements include: "There IS Evidence for God!" or "Beyond Reasonable Doubt Jesus is Alive!" or "War Divorce Wealth: What does Jesus say?" These are all intended to attract drivers. The phone number remains the same on all of them (83) FOR-TRUTH; then, in the left corner their logo and on the right, a biblical citation.

What is striking is how many of their billboards reference the Gospel of John: for example, their "Christians & Politics: What does Jesus Say?" includes the citation John 18:36 where Jesus says "My kingdom is not from this world."

FIGURE 6.2. Billboard, Christian Aid Ministries; I85 Southbound, North Carolina. Credit: Author.

After noticing this particular billboard several times along the southbound route of I-85 in North Carolina, I decided to call the number because I wanted to learn more about their understanding of the Gospel of John. When I called, a kindly man named Roger answered the phone, and I asked about their interest in the Gospel of John. Roger told me that the Gospel of John has the most famous verse in all of the Bible—John 3:16—and he proceeded to quote it. Then I asked about John 18:36, the citation I had seen on the Christians & Politics billboard, and he told me that it was important for Christians not to get caught up in politics these days; politics in this world are divisive, he said. What Jesus says in John 18:36 ("my kingdom is not from this world") means that Christians should focus on Jesus's kingdom, the kingdom of Heaven, the kingdom of God. What's striking about these billboards is that they do not include any full verses from the Bible: their intention, rather, seems to be to get drivers to see a scriptural citation and then to follow up by reading the passage itself. It's easy to miss the citation entirely because it is printed with such a small font; the billboards work by their sheer affective potency: curious drivers will hopefully want to learn more, it seems.

I asked Roger about Christian Aid Ministries' interest in humanitarian work. Although he did not mention any biblical references specifically, there are several themes in the Gospel of John that have been used to support Christian faith-based humanitarian organizations. For example, the Fourth Gospel contains striking images of Jesus as the good shepherd: after saying that the one who enters the sheepfold through the gate "is the shepherd of the sheep" who "calls his own sheep by name and leads them out," and the sheep follow him, Jesus shifts to explaining who he is: "I am the gate for the sheep," Jesus says, "I am the good shepherd. The good shepherd lays down his life for the sheep" (John 10:7, 11). One of the most ubiquitous images from early Christian art is that of Jesus as the Good Shepherd. Of course, the image is not exclusively Johannine. Luke 15, for example, contains the parable of the lost sheep and the person who finds it and "lays it on his shoulders." Matthew's Jesus speaks about "the Son of Man" who "will separate people one from another as a shepherd separates the sheep from the goats" (Mt 25:31–32). Among the early depictions of Jesus in Christian art, many seem to have Jesus as the Good Shepherd in mind: above the third-century baptismal font in the Church at Dura Europus in Syria, for example, is an image of Jesus holding a ram on his shoulders and goats or sheep alongside his feet. Similar figures frequently appear in frescos on the wall of the catacombs in Rome.[22] Today, visitors to Jerusalem can purchase a "Good Shepherd" statue carved in olive wood, prepared with John 10 explicitly in mind.

We know that early Christian writers linked Psalm 23, which begins with "The Lord is my shepherd," to the Johannine images of Christ as the good shepherd and to the title "lamb of God" that is unique to John. In the interpretations of these images from John's Gospel, Jesus can be both shepherd and lamb, as both Augustine and Chrysostom suggested in the fourth and fifth centuries: "As the Good Shepherd," Jennifer Freeman writes, "who was also paradoxically also the sacrificial lamb Jesus embodied power in powerlessness. . . . Jesus invoked the long history of the philanthropic shepherd while transforming its very image in his likeness."[23] By tying the image of the Good Shepherd to ancient philanthropy, as

FIGURE 6.3. Good Shepherd, olive wood, Jerusalem. Credit: Author.

Freeman suggests, we find a striking contemporary resonance, one that joins yet another story unique to the Fourth Gospel.

John's Gospel is the only one to include the following exchange between Jesus and Simon Peter:

> When they had finished breakfast, Jesus said to Simon Peter, "Simon son of John, do you love me more than these?" He said to him, "Yes, Lord; you know that I love you." Jesus said to him, "Feed my lambs." A second time he said to him, "Simon son of John, do you love me?" He said to him, "Yes, Lord; you know that I love you." He said to him the third time, "Simon son of John, do you love me?" Peter felt hurt because he said to him a third time, "Do you love me?" And he said to him, "Lord, you know everything; you know that I love you." Jesus said to him, "Feed my sheep." (John 21:15–17)

Countless faith-based organizations have used the Johannine phrase "feed my sheep" as a kind of call to feed those who are hungry; soup kitchens, food banks, and deliveries of food shipped around the world draw from John's distinctive images. There is a legacy of the Fourth Gospel that has flourished in social justice movements against slavery, poverty, hunger, and oppression. Of course, in many cases, these food missions are also an opportunity to missionize, to make new converts to Christianity. And here the double-edged sword of colonialism and its legacies, and of the proselytism baked into Christianity from its beginnings, reveals again John's varied legacies.

Conclusion

This chapter has provided an opportunity to reflect on how the Fourth Gospel inspires diverse American movements, especially around themes of evangelism. John's Gospel may seem an unlikely source for evangelicals; after all, it is the Gospel of Matthew that concludes with Jesus saying: "Go therefore and make disciples of all nations, baptizing them in the name of the Father and of the Son and of the Holy Spirit" (Mt 28:19). This passage, also found in the longer ending of the Gospel of Mark, is a rallying cry for Christian missionaries. But it is John 3:16 that serves to unify Christians of various denominations; the verse continues to offer evangelical Christians a creed, a hinge on which all other beliefs depend.

7

"The Disciple Whom Jesus Loved"

THE MYSTERY OF THE BELOVED DISCIPLE

CHRISTIANITY IS a scriptural religion: it has a sacred text—the Bible—and now nearly two thousand years of interpretations of that text. And yet it is incredibly diverse: different branches of Christianity like the Roman Catholic, Eastern Orthodox, and Protestant all recognize the twenty-seven books of the New Testament as sacred, but they differ in their canons of the Old Testament. But to look at the history of interpretation among the denominations and forms of Christianity reveals a dizzying world of diverse interpretations. The hermeneutical landscape is a bewildering forest of diverse voices, approaches, and interpretations. This is how scriptural religions work, at least in part; the sheer elasticity of texts, the ongoing debates about their meaning, the constant return to the sacred text in search of "the truth"—these are essential to what it means to hold scripture in such high regard.

One fascinating way to observe the endless expanse of scriptural interpretation is to consider the accretions of meanings, the selective use of particular passages, and above all the way that biblical stories morph and change over time as they are told and retold, interpreted and reinterpreted. Scripture is surprisingly malleable. In this chapter, I want to look at the stories about the "beloved disciple" in the Fourth Gospel and the figure's afterlives, which will also take us into the figure of Mary Magdalene, the story of the adulterous woman in the Gospel of John, and the curious conflations of stories that facilitate creative uses of the Fourth Gospel in contemporary fiction.

The Beloved Disciple

The mysterious figure of the "beloved disciple" is unique to John's Gospel, where the character is mentioned some six times as "the one whom Jesus loved." In the last of these instances, the figure is credited with having written the Gospel itself. The first mention of the character comes after the story of Jesus washing the feet of his disciples. Afterward, Jesus foretells his betrayal, and then the narrator writes: "The disciples looked at one another, uncertain of whom he was speaking. One of his disciples—*the one whom Jesus loved*—was reclining next to him; Simon Peter therefore motioned to him to ask Jesus of whom he was speaking. So while reclining next to Jesus, he asked him, 'Lord, who is it?' " (Jn 13:22–24). The figure appears again as Jesus is dying on the cross: he looks at those standing nearby, and "when Jesus saw his mother and *the disciple whom he loved* standing beside her, he said to his mother, 'Woman, here is your son.' Then he said to the disciple, 'Here is your mother.' And from that hour the disciple took her to his own home"

(Jn 19:26–27, emphasis added). To add to the complexity of Jesus's emotion toward the figure, the first of these passages uses the Greek verbal form of *agapē,* a word that could mean "affection" and "love," while the second uses *filia,* which tends to mean something more like "friendship." It's impossible to know whether the use of different terms holds significance, because the terms in ancient Greek were frequently used interchangeably. But subsequent speculation about the identity of the figure as well as his precise relationship to Jesus draws upon different nuances to the terms for love.

The beloved disciple's remaining appearances are found in the stories of the empty tomb and in the final chapter of the Fourth Gospel. In the story of the empty tomb in the Gospel of John, for example, the character appears in the scene where Mary Magdalene reports the empty tomb to Jesus's disciples (emphasis added in the following examples):

> Early on the first day of the week, while it was still dark, Mary Magdalene came to the tomb and saw that the stone had been removed from the tomb. So she ran and went to Simon Peter and the other disciple, *the one whom Jesus loved,* and said to them, "They have taken the Lord out of the tomb, and we do not know where they have laid him." (Jn 20:1–2)

In chapter 21, the raised Jesus appears to the disciples at the Sea of Tiberias,

> Just after daybreak, Jesus stood on the beach; but the disciples did not know that it was Jesus. Jesus said to them, "Children, you have no fish, have you?" They answered him, "No." He said to them, "Cast the net to the right side of the boat, and you will find some." So they cast it, and now they were not able to haul it in because there were so many fish. That

> *disciple whom Jesus loved* said to Peter, "It is the Lord!" (Jn 21:4–7)

And finally, at the very end of the Gospel of John, we find this passage, one that we looked at briefly in the introduction:

> Peter turned and saw *the disciple whom Jesus loved* following them; he was the one who had reclined next to Jesus at the supper and had said, "Lord, who is it that is going to betray you?" When Peter saw him, he said to Jesus, "Lord, what about him?" Jesus said to him, "If it is my will that he remain until I come, what is that to you? Follow me!" So the rumor spread in the community that *this disciple* would not die. Yet Jesus did not say to him that he would not die, but, "If it is my will that he remain until I come, what is that to you?" *This is the disciple* who is testifying to these things and has written them, and we know that his testimony is true. (John 21:20–24)

The images we find in each of these passages about the "disciple whom Jesus loved" are both intimate and mysterious. One wonders whether the author of John thought readers would instantly know who the figure was, or whether there was a particular reason to obscure the character's identity. The beloved disciple has had a long and complex history, beginning at the very start with the Fourth Gospel.

The identification of John, the son of Zebedee, one of Jesus's twelve disciples, as the "one whom Jesus loved" and the author of the Fourth Gospel has been held since as early as the second century.[1] Irenaeus, for example, identified John as the beloved disciple and the author of the Gospel in the late second century. After mentioning Matthew, Mark, and Luke as writers of Gospels, he says, "Afterwards, John, the disciple of the Lord, who also had leaned upon his breast, did himself publish a Gospel during his residence at Ephesus in Asia" (*Against Heresies* 3.1.1). Note here that the translation "leaned upon his breast" is a common translation for the Greek "reclining next to Jesus." Eusebius, the first church historian, writing in the early fourth century follows Irenaeus, and thereafter the identification of the beloved disciple as John, the Son of Zebedee, and the author of the Fourth Gospel became cemented in the tradition.

Many artistic renderings of the crucifixion scenes incorporate the image of John, the son of Zebedee, as the Jesus's beloved disciple, the Evangelist. Take, for example, the sixteenth-century Spanish sculptor Juan de Balmaseda, whose "Lamentation of Christ" depicts three grieving figures around Christ's body, which has been removed from the cross but still bears the wounds of the nails. On the left, with his arms coiled through Jesus's arms, holding him up, is John the Evangelist; here it is almost the reverse of the beloved disciple reclining next to Jesus or leaning on his breast: Jesus seems to be reclining toward John, and resting on the lap of the central figure behind him, Mary the mother of Jesus. To the right, Mary Magdalene, dressed in gold, holds Mary the mother's hand and looks upward, toward the heavens. It's a curious image and one that derives at least in part from a reading of John 19 where Mary Jesus's mother, Mary Magdalene, Mary the wife of Clopas, and the disciple "whom Jesus loved" grieve beside the cross.

Such artistic renderings of the scenes of Jesus at or following his death are not particular to western visual traditions. North Carolina Museum of Art's collections include a particularly fine example of an Egyptian Coptic icon in triptych form (three panels). Made in the twentieth century, the piece offers a central panel with Jesus on the cross, and on the two side panels the images of those who were crucified with him. Looking

FIGURE 7.1. Coptic artist, Crucifixion Triptych, Tempera and gold leaf on wood panel. Credit: North Carolina Museum of Art, Raleigh. Gift of Dr. R. T. K. Scully, 2019.18.

closely at the main panel, we can see two figures, one on either side of the cross, and above them, Arabic writing that identifies who the figures are: on the left, the translation of the text is "the one who bore God" (i.e., Mary, the Mother of God, as she was called since at least the fourth century), and on the right the text reads "John the beloved." Icons have long been a part of Christian worship; used in multiple ways in churches and in private homes, these images are imbued with sacred meaning. The viewer of this triptych, and perhaps those who encountered it first in a religious context in a Coptic church, would have recognized the figures on either side of Jesus as Mary and the Beloved Disciple who took her in after Jesus's death.

In the Fourth Gospel, the beloved disciple is always spoken of in third person. He is, according to Adele Reinhartz, "the implied author, the one whose witness is preserved in the book, whose words are recorded, and therefore whose point of view is represented throughout, as the one who has determined what to exclude as well as what to include."[2] Raymond Brown suggested that not only is the beloved disciple the implied author, but also that he was a key figure from the beginnings of the Johannine community: "During his lifetime," Brown writes, "whether in the period of Jesus's ministry or in the post-resurrectional period, the Beloved Disciple lived through the same growth in Christological perception that the Johannine community went through, and it was this growth that made it possible for the community to identify him as the one whom Jesus particularly loved."[3]

The ambiguity of the character and the nature of his relationship to Jesus has led to various theories and wild speculations. There is simply no solid evidence for determining whether the "beloved disciple" was an actual person; if an actual person, who exactly; and, if an actual person, what the individual's role was in writing the Gospel. Some have claimed that the beloved disciple was actually Thomas (yes, doubting Thomas) and others have claimed that it was Lazarus.[4] We don't need to belabor the topic here; the scholar Tom Thatcher presents a current consensus—namely, that the character of "the Beloved Disciple" is "a historical figure whose presentation in the Fourth Gospel reflects his legendary status as the source of the Johannine tradition."[5] The "beloved disciple," then, is a person who played an important role in the development of the Johannine community, but may not have actually been the individual to write the Gospel itself.

The fact that we cannot know for certain who wrote the Gospel and who the "beloved disciple" was has led to a wide variety of creative interpretations. One of the earliest alternative suggestions—made obliquely to be sure—comes from the gnostic Gospel of Mary, which centers on Mary Magdalene as a teacher after Jesus's ascension. At the heart of this Gospel is a discussion between Mary and the other disciples, especially Peter. Peter says to Mary in this Gospel,

> "Sister, we know that the Savior *loved you more than all other women.* Tell us the words of the Savior that you remember, the things you know that we don't because we haven't heard them." Mary responded, "I will teach you about what is hidden from you." And she began to speak these words to them. (10,1–10, emphasis added)[6]

At the end of her teachings, the disciples begin to argue about the validity of what she had said. And Peter, in particular, questions her teaching, saying "Did he, then, speak with a woman in private without our knowing about it? Are we to turn around and listen to her? Did he choose her over us?" (17,10). Peter here seems to be astonished that Jesus would speak with a woman separately from the (male) disciples. After this Mary pleads with Peter: "Do you think that I have thought up these things by myself?" And then the disciple Levi steps in, saying:

> Peter, you have always been a wrathful person. Now I see you contending against the woman like the adversaries. For if the Savior made her worthy, who are you then for your part to reject her? Assuredly the Savior's knowledge of her is completely reliable. *That is why he loved her more than us.* (18, emphasis added)

It's impossible to know whether the author of the Gospel of Mary meant to reference the passages in the Gospel of John that mention the beloved disciple, but it is worth remembering that John was the Gospel especially favored by Christian gnostics. What is clear in the Gospel of Mary is that some early Christians seemed to have thought that Jesus had a special relationship to Mary Magdalene, and that she could be understood to be the one whom Jesus loved more than the other disciples—in other words, the beloved disciple.[7]

There is another text from the Nag Hammadi collection of gnostic books, the Gospel of Philip, that seems to suggest a similar idea. Although the text remains very fragmentary, it has not stopped contemporary speculation, as we will see. The relevant passage reads:

> The companion of the [Savior] is Mary of Magdala. The [Savior loved] her more than [all]the disciples, [and he] kissed her often on her [mouth]. The other [disciples] . . . said to him, "Why do you love her more than all of us?" The Savior answered and said to them, "Why don't I love you like her? If a blind person and one who can see are both in darkness, they are the same. When the light comes, one who can see will see the light, and the blind person will stay in darkness." (Gospel of Philip 63,30–64,9)

The allusion to Johannine language of light and darkness is clear here. But it's important to be cautious in interpreting what's happening in this passage: every word in brackets above has been reconstructed by editors, and the ellipsis means that a whole section has been lost. The fragmentary nature of the passage has not prevented fantastic theories, however, and we will return to that shortly. At the very least, we can see that some Christians (re)invented the beloved disciple as Mary Magdalene and, in so doing, subverted the tradition that John, the disciple and evangelist, was most beloved by Jesus.

We will return to Mary Magdalene later in this chapter, but in order to understand how the process of conflation works in Christian tradition and scriptural interpretation, I want to shift first to a story we have not yet examined: the story of the woman taken in adultery.

The Woman Taken in Adultery

One of the most famous stories from John's Gospel is that of the woman brought to Jesus with the charge of adultery. Let's begin with the story itself, long known as the *pericope adulterae*:

> Then each of them went home, while Jesus went to the Mount of Olives. Early in the morning he came again to the temple. All the people came to him and he sat down and began to teach them. The scribes and the Pharisees brought a woman who had been caught in adultery; and making her stand before all of them, they said to him, "Teacher, this woman was caught in the very act of committing adultery. Now in the law Moses commanded us to stone such women. Now what do you say?" They said this to test him, so that they might have some charge to bring against him. Jesus bent down and wrote with his finger on the ground. When they kept on questioning him, he straightened up and said to them, "Let anyone among you who is without sin be the first to throw a stone at her." And once again he bent down and wrote on the ground. When they heard it, they went away, one by one, beginning with the elders; and Jesus was left alone with the woman standing before him. Jesus straightened up and said to her, "Woman, where are they? Has no one condemned you?" She

> said, "No one, sir." And Jesus said, "Neither do I condemn you. Go your way, and from now on do not sin again." (Jn 7:53–8:11)

The history of this particular story is complex and begins with its very existence and placement in the Fourth Gospel. Recall that in chapter 2, we looked at the earliest handwritten copies of the Gospel of John and how each copy of John was in some sense unique because each copy was made by hand. What's striking about the *pericope adulterae* is that no early manuscripts of the Gospel of John include this story. The Bodmer Codex is our earliest copy of the full text of the Gospel of John and this pericope is nowhere to be found, for example. The same is true for other early copies. There are some literary allusions to the story—for example, by Origen, the third-century Christian philosopher and teacher—but nowhere is it directly attributed to the Gospel of John. What is notable, too, is that the first to incorporate the story in a copy of the Gospel of John appears to have been Jerome, who included the story in his Latin translation of the Bible in the late fourth century. In addition, Codex Bezae—the fifth-century bilingual (Greek and Latin) manuscript of the Bible—similarly includes the pericope in its transcription of the Gospel of John.

If you read versions of the New Testament like the New Revised Standard Version, you will find that there are brackets around the entire story, meant to indicate that there is doubt about whether the story was original to the Fourth Gospel. Some translators—including, interestingly enough, the *New World Translation* of the Jehovah's Witnesses—simply do not include the story at all. The lack of any early evidence for the *pericope adulterae* in the Gospel of John has led to what is now a growing, though still conjectural, consensus among scholars.

In their comprehensive study of the *pericope adulterae*, New Testament scholars Jennifer Knust and Tommy Wasserman, argue that "the story was interpolated [i.e., inserted] into a Greek copy of John in the West, probably during the first half of the third century, and with great care; that the Johannine pericope was then gradually but decisively brought into texts, liturgy, and art in Greek and Latin, albeit at different rates."[8] The late introduction of the story into the Fourth Gospel, however, does not mean that the story was not widely known, only that it was not attributed to the Gospel of John in the early period and was almost certainly not original to the Gospel. There is, indeed, strong evidence to suggest that Christians knew the story and that it seemed to have "a broad, if perhaps unexpected, appeal."[9]

One of the ways that stories work and perhaps the most important way they are kept alive and dynamic is in the oral retelling of them—from person to person, from preacher to congregation, from missionary to convert, and so forth. It is difficult, of course, to reconstruct the circulation of a story in oral form, especially from a distance of hundreds and hundreds of years. But one of the fascinating legacies of the story of the adulterous woman is the way it becomes conflated with other stories. Conflation—the blending of two or more texts, traditions, or stories into one—is important for understanding both the circulation of stories, their dissemination and transmission, and their many afterlives. In the case of early Christian stories, conflation often appears when writers use details from one Gospel alongside details from another and they blend them. In a contemporary nativity play today, for example, you might find both Magi and shepherds, even though the Magi are unique to Matthew's story and the shepherds are unique to Luke's version. This is also sometimes called harmonization: a preacher, for example, may know that each of these Gospels presents different details about Jesus's birth, but by adding in the details from both, the preacher effectively has harmonized them and erased their differences. Harmonization of the Gospels goes back to the very earliest period—at least as early as the second century.

If you have ever heard that Mary Magdalene was a prostitute, you have been a victim of conflation. Nowhere in any of the Gospels is Mary from the village of Magdala identified as a prostitute. Rather, she is one of Jesus's close followers, a witness to both Jesus's crucifixion and his resurrection.[10] But in the late sixth century, Pope Gregory I delivered a sermon on the Gospel of Luke 7:36–50, the story of a "woman in the city, who was a sinner," who came to Jesus and "stood behind him at his feet, weeping, and began to bath his feet with her tears and to dry them with her hair. Then she continued kissing his feet and anointing them with the ointment" (Lk 7:37–38); Jesus, in turn, forgives her sins. In John's Gospel, Mary the sister of Martha and Lazarus was "the one who anointed the Lord with perfume and wiped his feet with her hair" (Jn 11:2). But interestingly, John does not identify this Mary as "sinful." Mary and Martha are presented as devoted followers of Jesus, sisters of Lazarus, a family loved by Jesus. And then there is also Mary Magdalene in the longer ending of the Gospel of Mark who is described as the one "from whom he had cast out seven demons" (Mk 16:9). Gregory identifies all of these as the same Mary; in one fell swoop, Mary Magdalene has become the woman who had had seven demons, a sinful woman who anointed Jesus's feet with oil and perfume. It is only a short distance to Mary the prostitute, which becomes the dominant Christian and cultural tradition. It is based on a conflation of stories, aided by the frequency of the name "Mary" for different characters in the Gospels.

As we consider the afterlives of the Johannine stories of the beloved disciple, that of the adulterous woman, and that of Mary Magdalene, I want to turn now to two contemporary conflations (among many) in literature and film: the novels *The Last Temptation of Christ*, written by Nikos Kazantzakis, and *The DaVinci Code*, written by Dan Brown—both of which were followed with cinematic versions.

Two Contemporary Novels and Films

The Greek writer Nikos Kazantzakis published *The Last Temptation of Christ* in 1955. It is a highly controversial retelling of the story of Jesus's crucifixion that depicts him as both divine and human, but in particular emphasizes Jesus's doubts about his identity and fears for his execution. The novel depicts a decidedly human Jesus. As Kazantzakis says in his prologue to the work: "This book is not a biography; it is the confession of every man who struggles."[11] Kazantzakis borrows from conflations of the stories of Mary already in existence. Here is how he imagines, however, the scene of what can only be the story of the adulterous woman:

> They heard voices and laughter from the direction of the vineyards. Two young, flushed carriers entered the yard. "Bad news, bosses," they shouted, splitting with laughter. "It looks like Magdala's risen up. The people have taken stones and are hunting their *mermaid* in order to kill her!" "What *mermaid*, lads?" yelled the treaders, stopping their dance. "Magdalene?" "Yes, Magdalene, bless her! Two mule drivers brought us the news as they went by. They said the bandit chief Barabbas—phew! All fear and trembling he is!—they said he left Nazareth and invaded Magdala yesterday, Saturday."[12]

The image here of Mary Magdalene as a "mermaid" is not arbitrary, in my view. Mermaids have long been associated with seduction and deception.

As the narrative continues, we learn that Barabbas has broken down the doors of Mary Magdalene's house in an effort "to find the lady in question and slaughter her." Judas, standing nearby,

> Stood in the doorway and listened. He heard voices and saw a cloud of dust rise up. Men were running; women were screaming, "Catch her! Catch her!" and before the three men had time to jump out of the wine press or old stuff-pockets to slide down from his platform, Magdalene, her clothes in rags and her tongue hanging out of her mouth, entered the yard and fell at old Salome's feet. "Help!" she cried. "Help! They're coming!" Old Salome took pity on *the sinner*. She got up, closed the window and told her son to bolt the door. "Squat down on the ground," she said to Magdalene. "Hide yourself." Mary the wife of Joseph leaned over and looked at this *woman who had gone astray,* looked at her with both sympathy and horror. None but honest women know how bitter and slippery honor is, and she pitied her. But at the same time this *sinful body* seemed to her *a wild beast, shaggy, dark and dangerous*. This beast had almost snatched away her son when he was twenty years old, but he had escaped by a hair's breadth.[13]

Notice is what is happening here: Mary Magdalene is identified as a sinner, first of all, and has a "sinful body." Both Mary the mother of Jesus and Salome—herself a character with multiple afterlives—see her as sinful, but Mary adds that she is also a sinner who seems to be beast-like, "shaggy, dark and dangerous." Note what happens at the very end: Mary claims that

Mary Magdalene "had almost snatched away her son." The allusion to a special relationship between Mary and Jesus is conspicuous.

It would be far too simplistic to suggest that Kazantzakis has literally lifted material from the canonical Gospels as well as the noncanonical stories of Mary Magdalene being the disciple that Jesus loved, but this is how stories work—they are told and retold, they change over time. Stories can be conflated, can be molded and shaped, can be imagined in new ways.

At last, Barabbas, succeeds in finding Mary Magdalene:

> Barabbas ripped the house door off its hinges with one shove and seized Magdalene by her braids. "Outside, *whore*! Outside!" he roared, hauling her into the yard. The citizens of Magdala entered at this point. They grabbed her, lifted her up, brought her amidst books and fits of laughter to a pit near the lake, and threw her in. Then both men and women scattered all around and loaded their aprons and tunics with stones.[14]

At last Mary's identity as a "whore" becomes explicit. What follows is a struggle and a loud quarrel about whether she should be stoned or not—she was perhaps asking for mercy, was she not, they wonder? As the debate is about to turn violent, someone yells:

> "*Maran atha*! *Maran atha*!" he shouted. "The Lord is coming!" "Who's coming?" they all cried, circling him. "Who?" "The Lord," answered the youth, and he pointed behind him toward the desert. "The Lord—there he is!" Everyone turned. The sun was going down now; the heat was abating. A man could be seen climbing up from the shore. He was dressed all in white, like a monk from the monastery.[15]

At first, the "man in white" stops, fearing the "sight of the multitude." "I must leave! He said to himself, overwhelmed by the old fear." But Mary Magdalene cries out again, "Help!"

> The man in white heard the voice, recognized it and quivered. "It's Magdalene," he murmured. "Magdalene! I must save her!" He advanced rapidly toward the crowd, his arms spread wide. The more he approached the people and perceived their anger-filled eyes and the dark, tortured fierceness of their expressions, the more his heart stirred, the more his bowels flooded with deep sympathy and love. These are the people, he reflected. They are all brothers, every one of them, but they do not know it—and that is why they suffer. If they knew it, what celebrations there would be, what hugging and kissing, what happiness![16]

Barabbas rushes forward, stomps on her back, eager to kill her. But "Jesus restrained Barabbas's lifted arm."

> "Barabbas," he said, his voice tranquil and sad, "have you never disobeyed one of God's commandments? In your whole life have you never stolen, murdered, committed adultery or told a lie?" He turned to the howling multitude and looked at each person, one by one, slowly, "Let him among you who is without sin be the first to throw a stone!"[17]

Here there is an explicit quotation from John 8:7. And then in a final flourish as Barabbas apparently cannot be stopped, Judas steps forward and tells Barabbas to go home. The scene ends.

I've included this lengthy segment because it offers us a vivid retelling of the story of Mary Magdalene that is imaginative and creative, yes, but also engages with the history of conflations we have already seen. Kazantzakis does not shy away from a quotation from the Gospel of John ("Let him among you who is without sin be the first to throw a stone," Jn 8:7). And yet he takes tremendous license with the story, too, especially in the way he imagines characters like Barabbas. In the cinematic version of the novel, the scene ends with *Jesus* wiping the feet of Mary Magdalene—another kind of subversion, for it casts the story of the "sinful woman" who anoints Jesus's feet instead as Jesus wiping the feet of Mary Magdalene. What a striking reversal!

Another novel that reimagines the stories of the beloved disciple and Mary Magdalene is Dan Brown's *The DaVinci Code*. It begins with a fabulous claim to historicity:

> *FACT:*
>
> The Priory of Sion—a European secret society founded in 1099—is a real organization. In 1975 Paris's Bibliothèque Nationale discovered parchments known as *Les Dossiers Secrets*, identifying numerous members of the Priory of Sion, including Sir Isaac Newton, Botticelli, Victor Hugo, and Leonardo da Vinci. The Vatican prelature known as Opus Dei is a deeply devout Catholic sect that has been the topic of recent controversy due to reports of brainwashing, coercion, and a dangerous practice known as "corporal mortification." Opus Dei has just completed construction of a $47 million National Headquarters at 243 Lexington Avenue in New York City. All descriptions of artwork, architecture, documents, and secret rituals in this novel are accurate.[18]

The conceit of such an opening surely contributed to the controversies that the book inspired. Here in the *DaVinci Code*, Brown's story claims that the beloved disciple was none other than Mary Magdalene herself, perhaps in a borrowing from some of passages in the Gospel of Mary or the Gospel of Philip.

But the story is altogether fictitious, as Brown's characters—symbologist and scholar Robert Langdon from Harvard and Sophie Neveu, a young French cryptologist—investigate the mystery of the Holy Grail. Brown's story brings in perhaps the most famous painting of the Last Supper, that of Leonardo Da-Vinci, as evidence to show that the beloved disciple who was leaning on Jesus's breast at the last supper was a woman, Mary Magdalene. The novel recounts further that Jesus and Mary had a child together, and that Sophie Neveu—spoiler alert—is a descendant from this child's line.

Christian groups were vehemently opposed to these books and to the films that were based on them. Even though Kazantzakis was explicit that his was a work of fiction, Christians protested and condemned those who saw the films. But these books and their accompanying films offer us a contemporary window into the role of story, and the contentiousness of stories considered sacred. The outrage that Christians expressed about the books and films in many ways echoes early Christian worries about interpretation, concerns that persist in any scriptural religion. There are numerous cinematic productions of the Gospel of John, of stories of Jesus throughout the Gospels, and of creative approaches to the figure of Jesus that are not dependent on texts at all. Some have argued that Mel Gibson's 2004 *The Passion of the Christ* "is overwhelmingly Johannine in its depiction of Jesus's triumphant passion," though it imports many distinctive scenes found only in the Synoptics.[19]

Philip Saville's 2003 film *The Gospel of John* only uses words from the Gospel of John. Notably, it begins with several statements that suggest historicity, including: "Jesus and all of his early followers were Jewish. The Gospel reflects a period of unprecedented polemic and antagonism between the emerging Church and the religious establishment of the Jewish people."

This "polemic and antagonism," I would argue, is the *perspective* of the Fourth Gospel (though it never uses the term "Church"). When the first scene opens with a sunrise over a calm sea, the narrator begins with the opening of John: "In the beginning the Word already existed, the Word was with God, and the Word was God." The three-hour film at times invents characters, and Seville "attempts to keep his viewing audience's interest in the lengthy Johannine monologues by simply changing scenes."[20] This film, which purports to include only the words of the Fourth Gospel—which words? which version? we might ask—demonstrates that interpretation necessarily attends any reading of a text.

Conclusion

In many ways, that is the story of this book, too: when a story comes to be considered sacred it means that it matters; not only do the details of the story matter, but so too its interpretation. It's important to understand the meaning, important that the interpretation is correct. And yet over the course of two thousand years, Christians—in their many different perspectives and approaches, languages and cultures—have not always agreed on the sacrality of a story or the accuracy of its interpretation. Nor could they. That is what keeps a tradition alive: a return time and again to a story, finding new meanings, wrestling with those meanings, and seeing a story anew in every new place, new time, among new people and new circumstances.

Epilogue

ANY BIOGRAPHY of the Gospel of John will necessarily remain unfinished. The word "epilogue," in which the word "logos" is embedded, notwithstanding, John's legacy and its words do not exist only in the past or the present; they will continue well into the future. Its distinctive language and striking images, its contentious and controversial perspectives, its abstract poetry and narrative prose, the rich history of its interpretation—all of these features ensure that there will be no end to the Fourth Gospel's afterlives. For Christians, of course, it is a Gospel to be reckoned with, memorized and quoted, mined for its meanings. In its cultural appropriation, too, the Fourth Gospel and its legacy remain vibrant and alive.

I choose the word "remain" here deliberately, because one of the distinctive words that the Fourth Gospel uses—one we have yet to examine closely—is the seemingly ordinary word "remain," which comes from the Greek *menō*. It's a term with a wide semantic range: it can mean to stay, live, or dwell in a particular place; it can also mean stand fast or hold your ground, as in a battle; to stay or delay in a place, to tarry; it can be used for things that last, persist, stand the test of time, remain forever; to wait for someone or something; and it can mean to continue to stay close to a person or to an idea, to abide.

The Fourth Gospel uses the term when John the Baptist describes Jesus's baptism as the "Spirit descending from heaven like a dove, and it remained on him" (Jn 1:32–33). It's also used to talk about Jesus's movements: at Cana, for example, "Jesus and his disciples remain" for several days after Jesus changed the water into wine (Jn 2:12), and when Jesus learns that Lazarus is ill "he stayed two days longer in the place where he was" (Jn 11:6). But the majority of the uses of the word are more abstract, especially when Jesus uses it in his long discourses: "I have come as light into the world," he says, "so that everyone who believes in me should not remain in the darkness" (Jn 12:46). In his Farewell Discourse, the lengthy speech Jesus gives in chapters 14–17, Jesus urges listeners to abide in him, saying:

> *Abide* in me as I abide in you. Just as the branch cannot bear fruit by itself unless it *abides* in the vine, neither can you unless you *abide* in me. I am the vine, you are the branches. Those who *abide* in me and I in them bear much fruit, because apart from me you can do nothing. Whoever does not *abide* in me is thrown away like a branch and withers; such branches are gathered, thrown into the fire, and burned. If you *abide* in me, and my words *abide* in you, ask for whatever you wish, and it will be done for you. (Jn 15:5–8)

The metaphorical language here—Jesus as the vine, his disciples as the branches—is distinctly Johannine, as is the idea of abiding in him. What does it mean for Jesus to ask his disciples to abide in him? In part to stay the course, to keep close to him, and to give his words an important place within and among themselves, to keep his words at hand. These are ideas that stand in paradoxical tension with the history of the Gospel of John, for we have seen just how much the words of this Gospel can be understood so differently across time and place, and that they far exceed the boundaries of a book. We might think that the words at least remain, but our attention to the manuscript tradition, the translation history, and the diverse interpretations shows us that even the words themselves are malleable. Words can be changed.

The King James Bible, the English translation of the Bible made in the early seventeenth century during the English Reformation, continues to be the most widely used English translation. It is also the translation used most frequently in choral compositions. But there were earlier English translations, and the biblical scholar William Tyndale's is one of them. The sixteenth-century English composer Thomas Tallis used Tyndale's translation for his well-known anthem, "If ye love me," taken from the words of John's Gospel (14:15–16):

> If ye love me, keep my commandments,
> And I will pray the Father,
> And he shall give you another comforter,
> That he may *abide* with you forever,
> E'en the spirit of truth.

This four-part choral work is surprisingly simple and resonant in its harmonies, but the ideas contained in the passage return us again to Johannine paradoxes: Jesus insists that his followers show their love for him by keeping his commandments, he asks them to abide in him, and he promises them a comforter, an advocate, who will remain with them. And yet the subsequent history of the Gospel demonstrates just how elusive the sense of "abiding" really is. Christians could not agree on Jesus's words, or what he meant by them; they frequently found suffering far more constant than the presence of a "comforter."

Two new translations of the Gospel of John appeared in 2021, soon after the COVID-19 pandemic began. The Quaker scholar and translator Sarah Ruden begins her translation of the Gospel of John with "At the inauguration was the true account, and this true account was with god, and god was the true account" (Jn 1:1). And she translates the passage from John 14: "If you love me, you will guard and carry out my commands. And I'll ask the father, and he will give you another advocate, so that he'll be with you for all time" (Jn 14:15–16).[1] The other translation that appeared that year was the *First Nations Version: An Indigenous Translation of the New Testament*. It begins:

> Long ago, in the time before all days, before the creation of all things, the one who is known as the Word was there face to face with the Great Spirit. This Word fully represents Creator and shows us who he is and what he is like. He has always been there from the beginning, for the Word and Creator are one and the same. (Jn 1:1–2)[2]

At John 14, the First Nations Version reads: "If you love me, you will walk in my ways. I will ask the Father to send one who will always walk beside you and guide you *on the good road*" (Jn 14:15–16; italics included).

Look at these surprisingly different translations: "at the inauguration of the true account," writes Ruden; "Long ago, in the time before all days," says the First Nations Version. It is not simply that the words are utterly different, their meaning is, too. We might here add one more rendition of the words, found in N. Scott Momaday's novel *House Made of Dawn*. Here the "Priest of the Sun" preaches on John's opening verse:

> "In the beginning was the Word . . ." Now what do you suppose old John *meant* by that? That cat was a preacher, and, well, you know how it is with preachers; he had something big on his mind. Oh my, it was big; it was the *Truth,* and it was heavy, and old John hurried to set it down. And in his hurry he said too much. "In the beginning was the Word, and the Word was with God, and the word was God." It was the Truth, all right, but it was more than the Truth. The Truth was overgrown with fat, and the fat was God. The fat was *John's* God, and God stood between John and the Truth. . . . "In the beginning was the Word . . ." And, man, right then and there he should have stopped. There was nothing more to say.[3]

In this fictional account, the words of this Gospel should have ended with "In the beginning was the Word"—these six words would have been entirely sufficient to convey "the Truth."

As this book has shown, the rich history of the Gospel of John demonstrates just how elastic, how wide-ranging the understanding of its words and its very translation can be. This is how it has always been with sacred scriptures: what may seem like a simple beginning to the Gospel—in Greek just two words, in English "in the beginning"—takes interpreters into wholly new possibilities. The words are made endlessly alive by those who read them and see in them something new. The words may remain, frequently in altered forms, but the work of interpretation is always dynamic and forever finding new worlds of meaning.

ACKNOWLEDGMENTS

SOME OF the ideas in this book go all the way back to my undergraduate days, when I wrote my thesis on "the Jews" in the Gospel of John. I'm grateful to my advisor, Vernon Faillettaz, who instilled in me a love of close reading. I wish he were still here to read this book. When I decided to pursue a graduate degree in ancient Mediterranean religions, I thought I might continue along similar lines, and my graduate advisor Bart D. Ehrman and I continue to joke about this possibility. I'm grateful he didn't hold me to my initial proposal and for grounding my work in textual criticism and the many ways that words matter in the study of the ancient world.

More recently, I'm grateful for the Henry Luce Senior Fellowship at the National Humanities Center in Durham, NC, where I wrote much of this book; the collegiality among fellows, the tireless work of the librarians and other staff, and time and space to write in a beautiful setting made my work so much easier and enjoyable. Over the years, and especially during my time at the NHC, friends and colleagues have read drafts, provided helpful insights, offered suggestions about visual sources. Thanks especially to Joel Elliott, Georgia Frank, Sonia Hazard, Hilde Hoogenboom, Robin Jensen, Mark Cruse, AnneMarie Luijendijk, and Hugo Méndez. Thanks to my uncle, Larry Miller, for putting me in touch with Arnold Snyder, who helped me with some questions about the Anabaptists. I'm also grateful to my hosts in North Carolina, Ron and Lorisa, who gave me a sense of home away from home; and to Nan, for all our walks and talks. To my dear LHFers, with whom I shared some of this book, thank you. Your enthusiasm buoyed me up.

Warm thanks to Fred Appel at Princeton University Press for including this book in the Lives of Great Religious Books series. And to Fred and all of those at the press for shepherding this book through the gate and out into the world, thank you. I appreciate, too, the thoughtful and perceptive comments provided by two anonymous readers.

My parents gave me a childhood that made this book (remotely) conceivable: tromping around archaeological sites, driving through Kafr Kenna and Deir Hanna on so many occasions, visiting the traditional site of Lazarus's tomb—these kinds of experiences shaped this book in ways I can't express. I'm grateful to my father for reading a draft, and had my mother lived to read this book, I hope she would have been pleased. Thank you to my sister and brother with whom I continue to share memories and tell stories about our childhood in Nazareth. Finally, and always, my love and gratitude to John, Ben, Eli, and Olivia who make my life deeply meaningful and whole.

NOTES

Introduction

1. On early Judaism, Hellenism, and diaspora, see Martin S. Jaffee, *Early Judaism: Religious Worlds of the First Judaic Millenium* (Bethesda: University Press of Maryland, 2006), esp. 28–35.

2. Scholarship on the historical Jesus is extensive. For recent treatments of Jesus as an apocalyptic figure, see especially E. P. Sanders, *The Historical Figure of Jesus* (New York: Penguin Books, 1993); Bart D. Ehrman, *Jesus: Apocalyptic Prophet of the New Millenium* (New York: Oxford University Press, 1999).

3. For consistency throughout this book, unless otherwise indicated biblical quotations come from the New Revised Standard Version as found in Michael D. Coogan, ed., *The New Oxford Annotated Bible: New Revised Standard Version with Apocrypha* (New York: Oxford University Press, 2010).

4. See especially Bruce M. Metzger, *The Canon of the New Testament: Its Origin, Development, and Significance* (Oxford: Clarendon Press, 1987); Harry Y. Gamble, *The New Testament Canon: Its Making and Meaning* (Philadelphia: Fortress Press, 1985).

5. Robert Kysar, *John, the Maverick Gospel* (Louisville: Westminster John Knox Press, 2007 [c. 1976]), 2.

6. Jonathan Gottschall, *The Storytelling Animal: How Stories Make Us Human* (Boston: Houghton Mifflin Harcourt, 2012), 15.

7. Will Storr, *The Science of Storytelling* (London: William Collins, 2019), 2.

8. R. Alan Culpepper, *Anatomy of the Fourth Gospel: A Study in Literary Design* (Philadelphia: Fortress Press, 1983), 231.

1. "In the Beginning": The Making of the Gospel of John

1. For an overview of the issues related to dating, see Robert Kysar, "John, the Gospel of" in *The Anchor Bible Dictionary*, ed. David Noel Freedman, Vol. 3 (New York: Doubleday, 1992), 918–919.

2. Stephen G. Wilson, *Related Strangers: Jews and Christians 70–170 C.E.* (Minneapolis: Fortress Press, 1995), 71 and 294.

3. John Ashton, *Understanding the Fourth Gospel* (New York: Oxford University Press, 2007 [c. 1991]), 158.

4. See Shusaku Endo, *A Life of Jesus*, trans. Richard A. Schuchert (New York: Paulist Press, 1973), 32; see also R. S. Sugirtharajah, *Jesus in Asia* (Cambridge, MA: Harvard University Press, 2018), 224–248.

5. See, for example, Rudolf Bultmann, *The Gospel of John: A Commentary*, trans. G. R. Beasley-Murray (Philadelphia: Westminster Press, 1976), 113–115. For a more recent assessment of sources, see Michael Labahn, "Literary Sources of the Gospel and Letters of John," in *The Oxford Handbook of Johannine Studies*, ed. Judith M. Lieu and Martinus C. de Boer (Oxford: Oxford University Press, 2018), 23–43.

6. Wayne Meeks's article on this issue of the ascending and descending Christ in the Gospel of John has been highly influential: see his "The Man from Heaven in Johannine Sectarianism," *Journal of Biblical Literature* 91 (1972): 52.

7. On the story of doubting Thomas, see especially Glenn W. Most, *Doubting Thomas* (Cambridge, MA: Harvard University Press, 2005).

8. Labahn, "Literary Sources," 23; see also Robert Kysar "John, the Gospel of," in *The Anchor Bible Dictionary*, 920–922.

9. Raymond Brown, *The Community of the Beloved Disciple* (New York: Paulist Press, 1979), 17.

10. Brown, *The Community*, 22.

11. Brown, *The Community*, 23.

12. Hugo Méndez, "Did the Johannine Community Exist?," *Journal for the Study of the New Testament* 42 (2020): 367; see also Ashton, *Understanding the Fourth Gospel*, 22–33; see most recently, Christopher Seglenieks and Christopher W. Skinner, eds., *The Johannine Community in Contemporary Debate* (Lanham, MD: Lexington Books/Fortress Academic, 2024).

2. "Word Made Flesh": Encountering the Fourth Gospel as a Book

1. James Kugel and Rowan A. Greer, *Early Biblical Interpretation* (Philadelphia: Westminster Press, 1986), 36.

2. A lot has been written on ancient literacy in recent decades. The place to start is with William V. Harris, *Ancient Literacy* (Cambridge, MA: Harvard University Press, 1989); see also William A. Johnson and Holt N. Parker, eds., *Ancient Literacies: The Culture of Reading in Greece and Rome* (New York: Oxford University Press, 2009). For literacy and book culture in early Christianity, see Harry Y. Gamble, *Books*

and Readers in the Early Church: A History of Early Christian Texts (New Haven, CT: Yale University Press, 1995); Roger S. Bagnall, *Early Christian Books in Egypt* (Princeton, NJ: Princeton University Press, 2009); Kim Haines-Eitzen, *Guardians of Letters: Literacy, Power, and the Transmitters of Early Christian Literature* (New York: Oxford University Press, 2000).

3. This comes from a papyrus letter found at Oxyrhynchus in Egypt (*P.Oxy.* 2192). For an image of the letter and a brief discussion, see http://archive.csad.ox.ac.uk/POxy/VExhibition/2192.htm (accessed January 28, 2025); see also my *Guardians of Letters*, 77–85.

4. To read more about this, see Bart D. Ehrman, *Misquoting Jesus: The Story Behind Who Changed the Bible and Why* (New York: HarperCollins, 2005); see also D. C. Parker, *The Living Text of the Gospels* (Cambridge: Cambridge University Press, 1997); Bart D. Ehrman and Bruce M. Metzger, *The Text of the New Testament: Its Transmission, Corruption, and Restoration* (New York: Oxford University Press, 2005).

5. A useful introduction to palaeography in biblical manuscripts is Bruce M. Metzger, *Manuscripts of the Greek Bible: An Introduction to Greek Palaeography* (New York: Oxford University Press, 1981).

6. See especially the work of Colin H. Roberts, *An Unpublished Fragment of the Fourth Gospel in the John Rylands Library* (Manchester, UK: Manchester University Press, 1935), and *Manuscript, Society and Belief in Early Christian Egypt* (Oxford: Oxford University Press, 1979). The early dating of this fragment (and others) has been challenged most recently by Brent Nongbri in his book *God's Library: The Archaeology of the Earliest Christian Manuscripts* (New Haven, CT: Yale University Press, 2018).

7. The literature on early Christian monasticism is vast. A good place to start is William Harmless, *Desert Christians: An Introduction to the Literature of Early Monasticism* (New York: Oxford University Press, 2004); see also Peter Brown, *The Body and Society: Men, Women, and Sexual Renunciation in Early Christianity* (New York: Columbia University Press, 1988); Douglas Burton-Christie, *The Word in the Desert: Scripture and the Quest for Holiness in Early Christian Monasticism* (New York: Oxford University Press, 1993); Kim Haines-Eitzen, *Sonorous Desert: What Deep Listening Taught Early Christian Monks and What It Can Teach Us* (Princeton, NJ: Princeton University Press, 2022).

8. See https://codexsinaiticus.org/en/ (accessed May 20, 2025).

9. For images of these Bibles, see especially Christopher de Hamel, *The Book: A History of the Bible* (London: Phaidon, 2001) and *A History of Illuminated Manuscripts* (London: Phaidon, 1994); Michelle P. Brown, ed., *In the Beginning: Bibles Before the Year 1000* (Washington, DC: Smithsonian Institution, 2006).

10. The best academic introduction to New Testament versions is Bruce M. Metzger, *The Early Versions of the New Testament: Their Origin, Transmission, and Limitations* (Oxford: Clarendon Press, 1977).

11. David Parker, *Codex Bezae: An Early Christian Manuscript and Its Text* (Cambridge: Cambridge University Press, 1992); the quotation is taken from his description of the codex on the Cambridge University Library's website: https://cudl.lib.cam.ac.uk/view/MS-NN-00002-00041/1 (accessed May 31, 2025).

12. The manuscript has been digitized and available here: https://www.bl.uk/research/digitised-manuscripts/ (accessed January 29, 2025); see also Eleanor Jackson, *The Lindisfarne Gospels: Art, History & Inspiration* (London: British Library Publishing, 2022.

13. A. S. Hunt, ed., *The Oxyrhynchus Papyri*, vol. 8 (London: Egyptian Exploration Fund, 1911), no. 1151, 251–253; see more recently AnneMarie Luijendijk, "A Gospel Amulet for Joannia (P.Oxy. III.1151)," in *Daughters of Hecate: Women and Magic in the Ancient World*, ed. Kimberly B. Stratton and Dayna S. Kalleres (Oxford: Oxford University Press, 2014), 418–444; the translation provided here is taken from Luijendijk's article.

14. Luijendijk, "A Gospel Amulet," 421.

15. Robin M. Jensen, "The Gospel of John in Early Christian Art," in *The Edinburgh Companion to the Bible and the Arts*, ed. Stephen Prickett (Edinburgh: Edinburgh University Press, 2014), 132.

16. Robin Jensen, *Understanding Early Christian Art* (London: Routledge, 2000), 170; see also Philip F. Esler and Ronald A. Piper, *Lazarus, Mary and Martha: Social-Scientific Approaches to the Gospel of John* (Minneapolis: Fortress Press, 2006); J. Stevenson, *The Catacombs: Rediscovered monuments of early Christianity* (London: Thames andn Hudson, 1978).

17. For films, see Jeffrey L. Staley and Richard Walsh, *Jesus, the Gospels, and Cinematic Imagination: A Handbook to Jesus on DVD* (Louisville, KY: Westminster John Knox Press, 2007); for poetry that engages with the Gospel of John, see especially Thomas Gardner, *John in the Company of Poets: The Gospel in Literary Imagination* (Waco, TX: Baylor University Press, 2011).

3. "If You Know Me": The Divine Christ in Controversy

1. The literature on "Gnosticism" is vast; see especially David Brakke, *The Gnostics: Myth, Ritual, and Diversity in Early Christianity* (Cambridge, MA: Harvard University Press, 2010); John Harris, *Gnosticism: Beliefs and Practices* (Brighton: Sussex Academic Press, 1999); Karen L. King, *What Is Gnosticism?* (Cambridge, MA: Harvard University Press, 2005); Birger Pearson, *Ancient Gnosticism: Traditions and*

Literature (Philadelphia: Fortress, 2007); and Michael Allen Williams, *Rethinking Gnosticism: Arguments for Dismantling a Dubious Category* (Princeton, NJ: Princeton University Press, 1996).

2. Elaine Pagels, *Gnostic Gospels* (New York: Random House, 1979), xiii.

3. Karen L. King, *The Secret Revelation of John* (Cambridge, MA: Harvard University Press, 2006), 235.

4. Unless otherwise noted, the translation I am using here is from Marvin Meyer, ed., *The Nag Hammadi Scriptures: The Revised and Updated Translation of Sacred Gnostic Texts* (New York: HarperOne, 2007); there are multiple one-volume translations of the texts: see especially James M. Robinson, ed., *The Nag Hammadi Library* (San Francisco: HarperSanFrancisco, 1988); Bentley Layton, *The Gnostic Scriptures* (Garden City, NY: Doubleday, 1987); see also Willis Barnstone and Marvin Meyer, eds., *The Gnostic Bible: Revised and Expanded Edition* (Boulder, CO: Shambhala, 2009).

5. King, *The Secret Revelation of John*, 238.

6. On the later controversies about Origen, see especially Elizabeth A. Clark, *The Origenist Controversy: The Cultural Construction of an Early Christian Debate* (Princeton, NJ: Princeton University Press, 1992).

7. Elaine Pagels, *The Johannine Gospel in Gnostic Exegesis: Heracleon's Commentary on John* (Nashville: Abingdon Press, 1973), 13.

8. For the English translation, see especially Ronald Heine, ed., *Origen: Commentary on the Gospel of John*, 2 vols. (Washington, DC: Catholic University of America Press, 1989–1993).

9. Joseph Wilson Trigg, *Origen: The Bible and Philosophy in the Third-Century Church* (Atlanta: John Knox Press, 1983), 248.

10. Ehrman, *Misquoting Jesus*, 161–162.

11. Averil Cameron, *Christianity and the Rhetoric of Empire: The Development of Christian Discourse* (Berkeley: University of California Press, 1991), 65.

12. Trigg, *Origen*, 150.

13. William Lamb, "Johannine Commentaries in the Early Church," in *The Oxford Handbook of Johannine Studies*, ed. Judith M. Lieu and Martinus C. De Boer (Oxford: Oxford University Press, 2018), 427.

14. For the ways that the church fathers, including Augustine, interpreted scripture in the service of an ascetic agenda, see especially Elizabeth A. Clark, *Reading Renunciation: Asceticism and Scripture in Early Christianity* (Princeton, NJ: Princeton University Press, 1999).

15. John Rettig, *St. Augustine: Tractates on the Gospel of John*, Fathers of the Church series, volume 92 (Washington, DC: Catholic University of America Press, 1995), 11–12.

16. Rowan Greer, *Early Biblical Interpretation*, 198.

17. William Harmless, ed., *Augustine: In His Own Words* (Washington, DC: Catholic University of America Press, 2010), 159.

18. Harmless, *Augustine*, 159.

19. For the translation, see John Gibb and James Innes, *St. Augustin: Lectures or Tractates on the Gospel According to John* (Peabody, MA: Hendrickson, 1995; reprint of *Nicene and Post-Nicene Fathers*, first series, vol. 7 [1888]).

4. "Fear of the Jews": John and the Legacies of Antisemitism

1. Adele Reinhartz, "The Jews of the Fourth Gospel," in *The Oxford Handbook of Johannine Studies*, ed. Judith M. Lieu and Martinus C. de Boer (Oxford: Oxford University Press, 2018), 122.

2. Reinhartz, "The Jews of the Fourth Gospel," 122.

3. On the origin of Christian ideas about Satan, see especially Elaine Pagels, *The Origin of Satan: How Christians Demonized Jews, Pagans, and Heretics* (New York: Vintage, 1996).

4. April D. DeConick, "Why are the Heavens Closed? The Johannine Revelation of the Father in the Catholic-Gnostic Debate," in *John's Gospel and Intimations of Apocalyptic*, ed. Catrin H. Williams and Christopher Rowland (London: Bloomsbury T&T Clark, 2013), 151.

5. Adele Reinhartz, "'Children of the Devil': John 8:44 and its Early Reception," in *Confronting Antisemitism from the Perspectives of Christianity, Islam, and Judaism* (Berlin: De Gruyter, 2020), 48.

6. Quoted in Reinhartz, "'Children of the Devil,'" 48.

7. Kathleen Gallagher Elkins, "The Jews as 'Children of the Devil' (John 8:44) in Nazi Children's Literature," *Biblical Interpretation* 31 (2023): 374–75.

8. Elkins, "The Jews as 'Children of the Devil,'" 385.

9. H. Croner, *More Stepping Stones to Jewish-Christian Relations: An Unabridged Collection of Documents 1975–1983* (Mahwah, NJ: Paulist, 1985), 32–33.

10. Elkins, "The Jews as 'Children of the Devil,'" 390; see also Reinhartz, "'Children of the Devil,'" on the Charlottesville march, 49.

11. See https://www.vatican.va/content/francesco/en/letters/2024/documents/20241007-lettera-cattolici-mediooriente.html (accessed January 15, 2025).

12. See especially Musa W. Dube and Jeffrey L. Staley, "Descending from and Ascending into Heaven: A Postcolonial Analysis of Travel, Space and Power in John," in the volume they edited together, *John and Postcolonialism: Travel, Space and Power* (London: Sheffield Academic Press, 2002), 5.

13. Mary Huie-Jolly, "Maori 'Jews' and a Resistant Reading of John 5.10–47," in Dube and Staley, *John and Postcolonialism*, 95.

14. Robert E. Van Voorst, *Readings in Christianity*, 2nd ed. (Toronto: Wadsworth, 2001), 120.

15. Christopher Tyerman, *The Crusades: A Very Short Introduction* (Oxford: Oxford University Press, 2004), 10.

16. Andy Alexis-Baker, "Violence, Nonviolence, and the Temple Incident in John 2:13–15," *Biblical Interpretation* 20 (2012): 80–81.

17. Katherine Allen Smith, "The Crusader Conquest of Jerusalem and Christ's Cleansing of the Temple," in *The Uses of the Bible in Crusader Sources*, ed. Elizabeth Lapina and Nicholas Morton (Leiden: Brill, 2017), 24.

18. Smith, "The Crusader Conquest," 31–32.

19. Smith, "The Crusader Conquest," 40–41.

20. Joshua Trachtenberg, *The Devil and the Jews: The Medieval Conception of the Jew and Its Relation to Modern Antisemitism* (New Haven, CT: Yale University Press, 1943), p. 11.

5. "The Truth Will Make You Free": The Fourth Gospel and the Reformation

1. Christopher De Hamel, *The Book: A History of the Bible* (London: Phaidon Press, 2001), 190.

2. This quotation appears in Luther's *Preface* to his German translation of the New Testament; it is also found in Hans J. Hillerbrand, ed., *The Protestant Reformation* (New York: Harper & Row, 1968), 42.

3. Van Voorst, *Readings in Christianity*, 166.

4. Richard Marius, *Martin Luther: The Christian Between God and Death* (Cambridge, MA: Harvard University Press, 1999), 146.

5. Hillerbrand, *The Protestant Reformation*, 42.

6. Martin Luther, "That Jesus Christ Was Born a Jew," in *Luther's Works*, ed. Walther I. Brandt, vol. 45 (St. Louis, MO: Fortress Press, 1962), 200.

7. See Eusebius, *Ecclesiastical History* I.2.4 and I.4.14.

8. Marius, *Martin Luther*, 372.

9. It's worth reading this treatise in full; access is available online: Luther, "On the Jews and Their Lies," 1543, translated by Martin H. Bertram, https://www.prchiz.pl/storage/app/media/pliki/Luther_On_Jews.pdf (accessed May 25, 2025).

10. John Jeffries Martin, *A Beautiful Ending: The Apocalyptic Imagination and the Making of the Modern World* (New Haven, CT: Yale University Press, 2022), 131.

11. Michael Marissen, *Lutheranism, Anti-Judaism, and Bach's St. John Passion* (New York: Oxford University Press, 1998), 23; see also Hans J. Hillerbrand, "Martin Luther and the Jews," in *Jews and Christians: Exploring the Past, Present, and Future*, ed. James H. Charlesworth (New York: Crossroad, 1990), 127–50; and Heiko A.

Oberman, *The Roots of Anti-Semitism in the Age of Renaissance and Reformation* (Philadelphia: Fortress Press, 1984).

12. John H. Yoder, trans. and ed., *The Legacy of Michael Sattler* (Scottdale, PA: Herald Press, 1973), 156.

13. Hillerbrand, *The Protestant Reformation,* 131 (emphasis added).

14. *Luther's Works,* vol. 23, *Sermons on the Gospel of St. John chapters 6–8,* ed. Jaroslav Pelikan (St. Louis, MO: Concordia Publishing House, 1959), 123.

15. Hillebrand, *The Protestant Reformation,* 110–112.

16. Marissen, *Lutheranism,* 20.

17. Quoted in Marissen, *Lutheranism,* 30.

18. Martin Geck, "Introduction" to Nikolaus Harnoncourt's recording of the *St. John Passion,* Concentus musicus Wien (Teldec, 1993), 15.

19. The English translation here is taken from Marrisen, *Lutheranism,* 40–70; see also Michael Marissen's translations online: https://bachcantatatexts.org/BWV245.1.htm (accessed February 4, 2025).

20. Wilfrid Mellers, *Bach and the Dance of God* (New York: Oxford University Press, 1981), 97.

21. Mellers, *Bach and the Dance,* 128.

22. Ruth HaCohen, *The Music Libel against the Jews* (New Haven, CT: Yale University Press, 2011), 101.

6. "You Must Be Born Again": John's Gospel Among American Evangelicals and Beyond

1. Sara Patterson, "Feeling the Word: Sensing Scripture at Salvation Mountain," in *The Bible in American* Life, ed. Philip Goff, Arthur E. Farnsley II, Peter J. Thuesen (New York: Oxford University Press, 2017), 316.

2. Patterson, "Feeling the Word," 321.

3. Matthew Avery Sutton, "Redefining the History and Historiography on American Evangelicalism in the Era of the Religious Right," *Journal of the American Academy of Religion* 92 (2024): 38; see also his book *American Apocalypse: A History of Modern Evangelicalism* (Cambridge, MA: Belknap Press of Harvard University Press, 2014).

4. See, for example, in his sermon delivered in Pittsburgh in 1993: https://www.youtube.com/watch?v=ROCEHsiWD1A (accessed May 31, 2025).

5. Bryan Bibb, "Readers and Their E-Bibles: The Shape and Authority of the Hypertext Canon," in Goff et al, *The Bible in American Life,* 263.

6. Philip Goff, Arthur E. Farnsley II, and Peter J. Thuesen, "The Bible in American Life Today," in *The Bible in American Life,* 9.

7. Dwight Lyman Moody, "On Being Born Again," in *American Sermons: The Pilgrims to Martin Luther King Jr,* ed. Michael Warner (New York: Library of America, 1999), 678.

8. On American Fundamentalism, see especially George Marsden, *Fundamentalism and American Culture*, 3rd ed. (New York: Oxford University Press, 2022).

9. Richard Lyman Bushman, *Joseph Smith, Rough Stone Rolling: A cultural biography of Mormonism's founder* (New York: Knopf, 2005), 311.

10. Nicholas J. Frederick, "Of 'Life Eternal' and 'Eternal Lives': Joseph Smith's Engagement with the Gospel of John," in *Faculty Publications* 3619 (2015): 194–195.

11. See https://www.churchofjesuschrist.org/study/scriptures/jst/introduction?lang=eng (accessed May 31, 2025).

12. See https://www.churchofjesuschrist.org/study/scriptures/jst/jst-john/1?lang=eng (accessed May 31, 2025).

13. Frederick, "Of 'Life Eternal' and 'Eternal Lives,'" 204.

14. Frederick, "Of 'Life Eternal' and 'Eternal Lives,'" 207.

15. M. James Penton, *Apocalypse Delayed: The Story of the Jehovah's Witnesses* (Toronto: University of Toronto Press, 2015), 353.

16. Penton, *Apocalypse Delayed*, 249.

17. See the tract "Would You Like to Know the Truth?," https://wol.jw.org/en/wol/d/r1/lp-e/1102008390 (accessed January 20, 2025).

18. See https://wol.jw.org; *New World Translation* (accessed January 20, 2025).

19. Penton, *Apocalypse Delayed*, 251.

20. Mark A. Noll, *In the Beginning was the Word: The Bible in American Public Life, 1492–1783* (New York: Oxford University Press, 2016), 339.

21. See: https://christianaidministries.org/about/ (accessed February 23, 2025).

22. See Jensen, *Understanding Early Christian Art*, 37–41; see also Jennifer Awes Freeman, *The Good Shepherd: Image, Meaning, and Power* (Waco, TX: Baylor University Press, 2021).

23. Freeman, *The Good Shepherd*, 79.

7. "The Disciple Whom Jesus Loved": The Mystery of the Beloved Disciple

1. The British interpreter J. N. Sanders held that the beloved disciple was none other than Lazarus; recall that in the story of the raising of Lazarus, Mary and Martha send Jesus word that "he whom you love is ill" (Jn 11:3). See Sanders's *A Commentary on the Gospel according to St. John* (London: A&C Black, 1977), 31. So, too, interestingly enough, Ravi Ravinda's reading of John alongside Indian mysticism, takes this view and argues that the beloved disciple (i.e., Lazarus) is Jesus's "spiritual son" (*The Gospel of John in the Light of Indian Mysticism* [Rochester, VT: Inner Traditions, 2004], 221).

2. Adele Reinhartz, *Befriending the Beloved Disciple: A Jewish Reading of the Gospel of John* (London: Continuum, 2002), 23.

3. Brown, *Community*, 33.

4. Tom Thatcher, "The Beloved Disciple, the Fourth Evangelist, and the Authorship of the Fourth Gospel," in *The Oxford Handbook of Johannine Studies*, 89–90.

5. Thatcher, "The Beloved Disciple," 94.

6. The translation is Karen King's found in Meyer, ed., *The Nag Hammadi Scriptures*, although it is worth noting that the Gospel of Mary was not found among the Nag Hammadi codices; fragments of the Coptic and Greek texts were found elsewhere in Egypt.

7. On the relationship of the Gospel of Mary to the Gospel of John, and a translation compiled from the available fragments, see Karen L. King, *The Gospel of Mary of Magdala: Jesus and the First Woman Apostle* (Santa Rosa, CA: Polebridge Press, 2003), 129–133.

8. Jennifer Knust and Tommy Wasserman, *To Cast the First Stone: The Transmission of a Gospel Story* (Princeton, NJ: Princeton University Press, 2019), 343.

9. Knust and Wasserman, *To Cast the First Stone*, 343.

10. See further Bart Ehrman, *Peter, Paul, and Mary Magdalene: The Followers of History and Legend* (New York: Oxford University Press, 2008); Susan Haskins, *Mary Magdalen: Myth and Metaphor* (San Diego, CA: Harcourt, 1994).

11. Nikos Kazantzakis, *The Last Temptation of Christ*, trans. P. A. Bien (New York: Simon and Schuster, 1998 [c. 1960], 4.

12. Kazantzakis, *The Last Temptation*, 169 (emphasis added).

13. Kazantzakis, *The Last Temptation*, 170–71 (emphasis added).

14. Kazantzakis, *The Last Temptation*, 172 (emphasis added).

15. Kazantzakis, *The Last Temptation*, 174.

16. Kazantzakis, *The Last Temptation*, 175.

17. Kazantzakis, *The Last Temptation*, 176.

18. Dan Brown, *The Da Vinci Code: A Novel* (New York: Anchor Books, 2003), 1.

19. Staley and Walsh, *Jesus, the Gospels, and Cinematic Imagination*, 156.

20. Staley and Walsh, *Jesus, the Gospels, and Cinematic Imagination*, 146.

Epilogue

1. Sarah Ruden, *The Gospels: A new translation* (New York: Modern Library, 2021).

2. *First Nations Version: An Indigenous Translation of the New Testament* (Downers Grove, IL: InterVarsity Press, 2021).

3. N. Scott Momaday, *House Made of Dawn* (New York: HarperPerennial, 2018), 82. First published in 1966, I highly recommend reading Momaday's "Priest of the Sun" sermon on John 1:1 in full.

FURTHER READING

Handbooks, Commentaries, and Critical Studies

Ashton, John. *Understanding the Fourth Gospel.* New York: Oxford University Press, 2007.

Brodie, Thomas L. *The Gospel According to John: A Literary and Theological Commentary.* New York: Oxford University Press, 1993.

Brown, Raymond. *An Introduction to the Gospel of John.* New York: Doubleday, 2003.

Brown, Raymond. *The Community of the Beloved Disciple.* Mahwah, NJ: Paulist Press, 1979.

Bultmann, Rudolf. *The Gospel of John: A Commentary.* Philadelphia: Westminster Press, 1976.

Culpepper, R. Alan. *Anatomy of the Fourth Gospel: A Study in Literary Design.* Philadelphia: Fortress Press, 1983.

Dube, Musa W., and Jeffrey L. Staley, eds. *John and Postcolonialism: Travel, Space and Power.* London: Sheffield Academic Press, 2002.

Haenchen, E. *A Commentary on the Gospel of John,* 2 vols. Philadelphia: Fortress Press, 1984.

Keener, Craig S. *The Gospel of John: A Commentary.* 2 vols. Peabody, MA: Hendrickson Publishers, 2003.

Kysar, Robert. *John, the Maverick Gospel.* Louisville, KY: Westminster John Knox Press, 1976.

Lieu, Judith M., and Martinus C. de Boer, eds. *The Oxford Handbook of Johannine Studies.* New York: Oxford University Press, 2018.

Martyn, J. Louis. *History and Theology in the Fourth Gospel.* 3rd edition. Louisville, KY: Westminster John Knox Press, 2003.

Martyn, J. Louis. *The Gospel of John in Christian History: Seven Glimpses into the Johannine Community.* Paul N. Anderson, ed. Eugene, OR: Wipf & Stock, 2019.

Méndez, Hugo. *The Gospel of John: A New History.* New York: Oxford University Press, 2025.

Reinhartz, Adele. *Cast Out of the Covenant: Jess and Anti-Judaism in the Gospel of John.* Lanham, MD: Lexington Books/Fortress Academic, 2018.

Segovia, Fernando F., *The Farewell of the Word: The Johannine Call to Abide.* Minneapolis: Fortress Press, 1991.

Segovia, Fernando F., ed. *"What is John?," Volume II: Literary and Social Readings of the Fourth Gospel.* Atlanta: Scholars Press, 1998.

Seglenieks, Christopher, and Christopher W. Skinner, eds. *The Johannine Community in Contemporary Debate.* Lanham, MD: Lexington Books/Fortress Academic, 2024.

Talbert, Charles H. *Reading John: A Literary and Theological Commentary on the Fourth Gospel and the Johannine Epistles.* New York: Crossroad, 1992.

Reception and General History

Chafe, Eric. *J. S. Bach's Johannine Theology: The* St. John Passion *and the Cantatas for Spring 1725.* Oxford: Oxford University Press, 2014.

Farmer, Craig S. *The Gospel of John in the Sixteenth Century: The Johannine Exegesis of Wolfgang Musculus.* Oxford: Oxford University Press, 1997.

Felder, Cain Hope, ed. *Stony the Road We Trod: African American Biblical Interpretation.* Minneapolis: Fortress Press, 1991.

Goff, Philip, Arthur E. Farnsley II, and Peter J. Thuesen, eds. *The Bible in American Life.* New York: Oxford University Press, 2017.

Hamburger, Jeffrey F. *St. John the Divine: The Deified Evangelist in Medieval Art and Theology.* Berkeley: University of California Press, 2002.

Jensen, Robin M. *Understanding Early Christian Art.* London: Routledge, 2000.

Kugel, James L., and Rowan A. Greer. *Early Biblical Interpretation.* Philadelphia: Westminster Press, 1986.

Marissen, Michael. *Lutheranism, Anti-Judaism, and Bach's* St. John Passion. New York: Oxford University Press, 1998.

Mason, Emma, and Jonathan Roberts. *The Oxford Handbook of the Reception History of the Bible.* New York: Oxford University Press, 2013.

Noll, Mark A. *In the Beginning was the Word: The Bible in American Public Life, 1492–1783.* New York: Oxford University Press, 2016.

Nongbri, Brent. *God's Library: The Archaeology of the Earliest Christian Manuscripts.* New Haven, CT: Yale University Press, 2018.

Penton, M. James. *Apocalypse Delayed: The Story of the Jehovah's Witnesses.* Toronto: University of Toronto Press, 2015.

Staley, Jeffrey L., and Richard Walsh. *Jesus, the Gospels, and Cinematic Imagination: A Handbook to Jesus on DVD.* Louisville, KY: Westminster John Knox Press, 2007.

Staley, Jeffrey L. *Reading with a Passion: Rhetoric, Autobiography, and the American West in the Gospel of John*. New York: Continuum, 1995.

Sugirtharajah, R. S. *Jesus in Asia*. Cambridge, MA: Harvard University Press, 2018.

Sutton, Matthew Avery. *American Apocalypse: A History of Modern Evangelicalism*. Cambridge, MA: Harvard University Press, 2014.

Wilson, Stephen G. *Related Strangers: Jews and Christians 70–170 C.E.* Minneapolis: Fortress Press, 1995.

INDEX

Page numbers in italics refer to figures.

A NOTE ON THE TYPE

This book has been composed in Arno, an Old-style serif typeface in the classic Venetian tradition, designed by Robert Slimbach at Adobe.